Messengers of
Love, Light & Grace

Other Books by Terry Lynn Taylor

Messengers of Light

Guardians of Hope

Answers from the Angels

Creating with the Angels

Alchemy of Prayer

Angel Wisdom (with coauthor Mary Beth Crain)

Angel Courage (with coauthor Mary Beth Crain)

The Angel Experience

Messengers of Love, Light & Grace

Getting to Know Your Personal Angels

TERRY LYNN TAYLOR

An H J Kramer Book
published in a joint venture with
New World Library

Novato, California

An H J Kramer Book
published in a joint venture with
New World Library

Editorial office:
H J Kramer
P.O. Box 1082
Tiburon, California 94920

Administrative office:
New World Library
14 Pamaron Way
Novato, California 94949

Edited by Nancy Grimley Carleton
Text design and typography by Tona Pearce Myers
Interior illustrations by Marty Noble

Library of Congress Cataloging-in-Publication Data
Taylor, Terry Lynn.
Messengers of love, light, and grace : getting to know your personal angels /
Terry Lynn Taylor.
     p.   cm.
"An H J Kramer book."
Includes bibliographical references.
ISBN 1-932073-14-0 (pbk. : alk. paper)
1. Angels—Miscellanea. I. Title.
BL477.T395 2005
202'.15—dc22   2005014688

First printing, October 2005
ISBN-10: 1-932073-14-0
ISBN-13: 978-1-932073-14-X
Printed in Canada on acid-free, partially recycled paper.

Distributed to the trade by Publishers Group West

10 9 8 7 6 5 4 3 2 1

This book is dedicated to my dad, Gordon Taylor,
who died soon after I finished the first draft.
Anything good and true in me is because of him.
From him I learned how to look at the world through the
    eyes of a writer,
and how to cherish what is really important in life.
I thank the angels for bringing us together in this lifetime.

Contents

Introduction

Truth is a pathless land. (There is no need to seek it through any occult hierarchy, any guru, any doctrine....) The important thing is to free your mind of envy, hate, and violence; and for that you don't need an organization.

— J. KRISHNAMURTI

An epiphany is a sudden intuitive leap of understanding and consciousness, especially through an ordinary but striking occurrence. Twenty years ago, in 1985, I had an epiphany regarding angels that profoundly changed my consciousness and my life.

Before this epiphany occurred, I had recently made a commitment to *really* be a "spiritual person." I wanted to do it on my own terms, without an organization guiding me and without having to adopt a set of beliefs someone else had established. Something about Krishnamurti's statement "Truth is a pathless land" resonated with me. I had been a student of spiritual philosophy and meditation since 1973, but I felt that I hadn't integrated the underlying philosophy into my daily life. So I set out on a new regimen, one that would take my spirit above all the earthly hassles of being human. I changed my diet back to no meat, started to meditate and pray more regularly, and of course read a great many metaphysical books. But I found that I had tricked myself. I had given myself a set of beliefs — something I was trying to get away from — under the guise of being spiritual. Instead of creating joy and bliss, this new set of beliefs just resulted in hard work.

One day while doing my spiritual reading and feeling particularly frustrated, I came across the old Scottish saying "Angels can fly because they take themselves lightly." This simple saying hit my consciousness like a blast of light. The room I was sitting in sparkled and vibrated with light. I stopped reading and allowed a flood of exciting ideas and feelings to wash over me. Two very important insights occurred to me regarding my own spiritual quest. One, I was taking my life far too seriously, and spending too much time "trying" versus being, without respecting the lighter, more humorous side of God. Two, I was forgetting that angels are our spiritual helpers and personal guides in life. In my epiphany I experienced an expanded idea of what angels do and what they represent to us as spiritual beings having a human experience. Along with my expanded view of angels and divine humor came a deeper appreciation for life on earth and the importance of our human birth. Ironically the angels, who could be thought of as pure spirit, helped me begin to honor the importance of being human.

For as long as I can remember, I always knew that angels

existed and I always thought that they were a good idea. My philosophy was: Why question something that makes so much sense? As a teenager, I tended to be a bit reckless, and I had a friend who shared this tendency. I remember that each time we had a close call, we would comment that our guardian angels were probably fed up with working overtime. We also discovered that our guardian angels could do other special things besides saving us. We figured out that if we asked them, they would help us get what we wanted. When I look back at the silly things we asked for, I see how truly patient and loving God is.

After my epiphany, I began searching in earnest for books and other sources on angels and their ways. Whenever I met someone, I would ask, "Have you ever seen an angel?" or "Do you believe in angels?" I never got an outright no. Some people would say, "I don't know if I would call it angels, but I've had a few things happen that I just can't explain." At the same time, my close friend Shannon was having similar feelings about angels, and we would compare notes. Most of all, we discovered how interesting, fun, and light life can be when angels are around in full force.

During this time, I couldn't find a book on angels that resonated with my newfound joy, so I said to a friend, "I should just write my own book." My friend said, "That's actually a good idea!" I said I was just kidding, but as we discussed the idea further I realized the idea wasn't that far-fetched. I had been keeping a journal of my emerging angel consciousness and the little practices I had been doing, and it became the basis for my first book, *Messengers of Light*.

My inspiration for writing about angel consciousness comes from various sources: experiences, literature, and the people I meet. The main source I have used for all of the books I have written has been my strong intuitions regarding angels, which arise from a synthesis of all the outside information I've taken in and all the inner information I have from a deep sense of knowing. Of course, I ask the angels to inspire me at all times. I never feel I channel angels in the traditional sense (which is actually like taking dictation from spirits on the other side), because I've found that angels speak to us in feelings and guide us by inspiration. Most of all, angels give me the feeling that I'm not alone in the universe, and that I am eternally loved. Even when I feel as if the moral, intellectual, and spiritual lights are going out all around me, the angels remind me that the light is on in my heart, and in the hearts of many.

I am still exploring the basic questions that guided me in the beginning awakening of angel consciousness:

> What are the angels doing right now?
>
> What goes on in heaven that we need to be mindful of?
>
> How can we feel more at home being human?
>
> Can the angels help lead us to true happiness?
>
> Can we ask the angels for help on practical matters of living?

By working and playing with the angels, we make our way back to a natural and real experience of learning as much about love as we dare to while we are here on earth. The angels help us understand that we are called to love, and that we each have a unique way of expressing love.

Great experiences come when we take a risk and get past our fears so we can love deeply. Meaningful life experiences come from taking chances, not sitting back and thinking and wondering what it would be like, but getting out there and living our lives. Waking up and coming to our senses. What type of angel experiences are you cultivating? Calling forth? Going for? We have many experiences that are not tangible or physically measurable, yet they have a great power in influencing our lives. All of this needs to be factored into the mix.

I am often asked what my latest angel experience was. I always answer, "It is happening right now!" Now is your angel experience too, and the more you know the angels, the more multidimensional your angel experiences will be.

Our True Human Nature

We humans are amazing. We can reflect the light in ways that transform others, and we have our special talents, but we also stumble through life at the same time. One of the greatest aspects of angel consciousness is that it does not require you to be a saint, only good at heart. I am not a saint, and I don't care to be. My life has been an interesting journey, and I try not to judge where I end up as anything other than a set of experiences I am destined to encounter. I hope always to do my best. I've had the chance to shake hands with the Dalai Lama, and I've also shaken the hands of convicted murderers. In a humorous twist of fate, I have met almost every celebrity and spiritual teacher I idolized when I was young. They are as beautifully human as you or I.

My daily message to myself is simply to do my best and

stay connected to the angels. This looks different from day to day, depending on conditions, yet I know no other way to be. So, in my continuing journey to do my best, I offer this book to remind you that, no matter how dark it may seem here on planet earth, we are connected to heaven and there are multitudes of angels reminding us that we are loved unconditionally. There is still a great deal of fun to be had while we are here as earthlings.

This book represents a "best of" all the angel books I have written. I put "best of" in quotation marks because there is so much I wanted to include and share that it was difficult to know what was truly best. Basically I took previous writings I felt would help you stay inspired, sprinkled them with some new light, added some new writings, and put it all in one volume. I wrote my previous books in response to what I saw evolving when the angels alighted in people's lives, as well as what people were sharing with me in letters or at workshops about the way their lives were changing. For example, I wrote *Creating with the Angels* to help honor and encourage the newfound levels of creativity the angels were helping people with. I wrote *Angel Days* as a guided journal for igniting our faith anew each day.

All of the ideas and promptings the angels give to us are as vital to our spiritual survival today as they were ten years ago, at the peak of the popularity of angel books. I like to say that I write "human books," with the hope of encouraging and inspiring people to team up with the angels to make our human experience meaningful. I've come to the conclusion after all my years of spiritual investigation that there are no "spiritual people"; there is only Spiritual Law, which is the Light. Our true human nature is divine. All we need to do is be true to ourselves, and then it takes no effort for us to be spiritual.

Knowing Your Personal Angels by Heart

Blood must flow for the garden to flower.
And the heart that loves Me is a wound without shield.

— RUMI

When we connect with the angels on a conscious level, our hearts expand to allow for more love to come and go. Now we have a problem of sorts, because our hearts don't worry about breaking or fret about the pain involved when we suffer losses as a result of our loving. When feelings come from the heart, we don't need to argue with, intellectualize, or analyze them. Sometimes we make fun of people who "live in their hearts." Instead, we are wise to honor the parts of us that are heartfelt.

The heart is mysterious. It continues to mystify medical scientists as the main organ keeping us alive, and it confounds the best of us as the origin of love. Discoveries about how the electromagnetic field of the heart responds to emotional stimuli are giving us insight into how important love and relationships are to the health of the heart and body.

The heart is the most natural and organic part of us. When something is natural, it is uncorrupted and untouched — free to follow its own true course. The natural course for the heart is to love openly and freely. The heart is a connecting point for our relationship with God. It is the home of our true intentions, which is what God and the angels respond to. If your "heart is in the right place," God knows right where you are.

Knowing and Loving Yourself

Suppose I came along and handed you a clear glass vase and told you it was filled with an actual part of God. Inside this fragile vase you'd see a beautiful and unique color of light brought forth straight from the realm of heaven. After this special light entered the vase, the angels blessed it and carefully brought it to earth. Now you'd have the vase in your keeping. What would you do? This vase is priceless — so valuable you would never let it out of your sight or awareness.

Most likely you would cherish this vase of God light, and you would probably only let certain people near it. You would protect it from harm and make sure it didn't break. It would be the most important item to you because it represented a living spark of the light of God and you'd know that you were in charge of it.

Well, that is exactly what you are — a vessel of actual God light. How do we usually treat our unique vessels of God? Sometimes we forget we are made of God, and we are less careful with our special selves than we are with our material valuables. You are precious and priceless. God needs your light to shine brightly with love for your Self — for God.

Understanding fully who we are and what we are doing here involves being able and willing to love ourselves. This doesn't mean loving ourselves as soon as we do a few more things to make ourselves lovable; it means loving ourselves right now. We may ignore or deny this love, but the truth is we are always capable of loving ourselves at this very moment. Angels are intensely active in the lives of humans. Many people are seeking the spiritual dimension, and whether they realize it or not, they are attracting angels. The main lesson the angels have for us is that we are love, we are God on earth, and it is time to love ourselves and open our hearts.

Book Note

My plan of action for this book is to introduce the angels in chapter 1; invite them into our consciousness in chapter 2; cultivate the qualities that angels respond to and that help the planet heal in chapter 3; create a deep and meaningful relationship with the angels by integrating their spiritual help in practical, nurturing ways in chapter 4; awaken our prayer voice and send a joyful noise unto the Lord in chapter 5; learn from and be inspired by our fellow travelers in chapter 6; and tie up loose ends, go over issues that arise in our relationship with the angels, and explore being in the world but not of the world in chapter 7.

Remember, the angels are messengers. Their main message is of love, light, and grace. I pray you will be forever blessed with love in your heart, light in your mind, and grace in your soul.

CHAPTER ONE

Messengers of Light

To study angels is to shed light on ourselves, especially those aspects of ourselves that have been put down in our secularized civilization, our secularized educational systems, and even our secularized worship system. By secularization I mean anything that sucks the awe out of things.

— MATTHEW FOX, *THE PHYSICS OF ANGELS*

*I*n my first book, *Messengers of Light,* I discussed the many roles angels play in terms of the many halos, or hats, they wear. These halos represent the specific essences, spiritual expressions, or energies the angels are transmitting from God. Some of these expressions are very personal, as is the case with our guardian angels and spiritual guides. Some angels come to us in the moments when we need them the most, such as rescuers, healers, and miracle engineers. Other important angels embellish human life and help us experience meaning in our lives, such as happiness trainers and worry extinguishers.

The Halo of Messenger

The word angel *means messenger. An angel serves as an emissary of God, bringing the love of God into the world via person, word, object, or deed.*

It is rare that God just shows up through an unexplainable miraculous phenomenon. More often God works through people. If you look back on the wonderful things that have happened in your life, you will recognize that they usually showed up through a person, animal, or some form of God's creation. God works through the world.

— ALAN COHEN

The Hebrew word for angel is *malakh*, which means messenger. The Greek word for messenger is *angelos*. In both the New and Old Testaments of the Bible, there are many stories of angels appearing to humans bearing messages. These messages usually concern major events, for example, announcing the birth of the Messiah.

Because we don't always see and hear angels physically, we have to be especially creative and perceptive to receive our messages. Angels have ways of relaying messages we don't expect. Have you ever found yourself sitting for hours at a desk, racking your brain for the answer to a question or problem? Just as you decide to stop your pondering, perhaps a dove flies onto your windowsill. Noticing the dove gives you a sense of warmth and peace, and you find yourself walking toward the window. Then, as you look out the window, a truck goes by with words written on it that give you the answer you spent so much time trying to force out of your brain. As soon as you release the struggle, the message comes through effortlessly.

Pay attention to the subtleties in life. Angels have many ways of reaching us, but we often miss them. For example, a child, in a moment of spontaneity, may blurt out a statement for which only you know the meaning. While thumbing through a book, a page may fall open with a clear message in the print. Headlines in the newspaper, taken out of context, might contain your message. Angels with messages often appear to us in dreams. Angels are very creative in the ways they communicate with us; we need to be just as creative in listening for our messages.

Messages from heaven always come for the highest good of all concerned. If you receive messages or impressions that *seem* positive but don't *feel* positive, ask yourself, "Does this message resonate with unconditional love?" Usually, a very clear yes or no answer will come to you. Messages from heaven never urge force or domination. Detailed instructions, such as "Walk to the corner, buy some cigarettes, smoke one, then call your neighbor and tell him off," are generally not messages from heaven. Heavenly messages often take the form of "Don't worry.... Be creative.... Everything is all right.... All is well.... Forgive.... Trust...."

Angels inspire us through mystical insight and sudden brilliant, or even bizarre, ideas. Some of us experience angels as inner spiritual forces that guide our higher selves by instilling noble thoughts and ideals into our consciousness. All angels are messengers of some sort, regardless of the specific roles they play. Angels who are couriers of God have important news to carry. These messengers keep at you until you receive their news, so remember to relax, release, and let your intuition guide you.

The Halo of "Changel"

Since beginning to write about angels, I found I was using the word *change* a lot. Quite often I would automatically type an *l* at the end of the word, because of course I was so used to writing the word *angel*. I didn't think much about this at first, and actually found it a bit annoying, until I realized that this typographical error contained a message: Life is change and change is life, and angels are heralds of change. They can help us with changes big and small. So *changels* remind us to let go of the familiar and welcome the new — to accept the "facts" of life with an open heart. Aging is one of the areas where the changels really take charge. The following quotation sums this up for me.

> *On the whole, age comes more gently to those who have some doorway into an abstract world — art, or philosophy, or learning — regions where the years are scarcely noticed and the young and old can meet in a pale truthful light.*

> — FREYA STARK (1893–1993)

The Halo of Coach

One way to think of angels is as coaches in the game of life. Coaches don't necessarily play the game they are coaching, but they are still very important to the players. Coaches don't have to be able to play the game well themselves; they just need to understand human nature. Angels can serve as our private coaches by reminding us to include fun and happiness in our life games. Angels can coach us in bringing love, beauty, and peace into our lives. Angels cannot understand why more humans don't join in the divine cosmic dance of the universe. Angels and children get along well because children can readily play and have fun — and they do it with joy, singing, screaming, and laughing. Angel coaches teach fun and merriment.

At times angels envy us for being human. Angels admire the human ability to enter deeply into the passion of love — to have strong convictions from the heart. They envy our freedom of choice, known as free will. Free will gives us humans tremendous creative power. We have the capacity to create timeless gifts of art, literature, music, and great thinking to inspire the human race, even long after we are gone.

Years ago I coached a girls' basketball team. The girls were twelve and thirteen years old, and I found that when they took the game too seriously, they didn't have fun. As their coach, I told them that at their age basketball was meant to be fun. Regardless of whether we won a game or not, we were going to focus on being a team and enjoying what we were doing. So one of my rules was that if we lost a game we would cheer just as loudly as if we had won. I remember one game when we got slaughtered by a team that was very skilled but seemed lifeless. At the end of the game my girls jumped for joy, hugging one another and cheering, "Good game!" The other team stood stunned and confused, wondering if my team thought they had won. They did!

The Ever-Important Halo of Guardian

For He will give His Angels [especial] charge concerning you,
To guard you in all your ways.

— PSALMS 91:11

A guardian angel is assigned to each person on earth. Each human being, regardless of belief, status, shape, or size, has the privilege of having a guardian angel. Your guardian angel is with you all the time, wherever you go, whatever you do. It has been said that when God looks at you God sees two — you and your guardian angel. When a French farmer traveled a road alone and met up with another single traveler, the two travelers would greet each other by saying, "Good day to you and your companion" (companion meaning guardian angel).

Your guardian angel has been with you throughout time and was there when you decided to come into this world as the special human you are today. Your guardian angel remembers and keeps track of the noble goals you set for yourself, the high aspirations you have stored deep within your unconscious mind.

My first memory of my guardian angel goes back to when I was three years old. I was playing in an off-limits area in our backyard with one of my teddy bears. Somehow, the teddy bear fell down a ravine. I stood looking at it for a minute, trying to decide whether to forget it or go and get it. I decided to go and get it because it was the smallest bear in my collection and therefore important. I took one step toward the ravine and heard a voice say, "No, don't go down there; leave the teddy bear and go back up to the house." I remember feeling as if there were a barrier between me and the ravine. Considering that I wasn't supposed to be there in the first place, I left and went back up to the house with only the memory of my teddy bear. I remember thinking that he would make friends with some little animals and everything would be okay.

You may remember a time in your life when you were reckless and could have been seriously hurt, and it seemed as if an invisible force pulled you to safety. Maybe you don't have a story like this yourself but have heard one or read one somewhere. Guardian angels are known to most of us who drive cars, especially on the freeway. Basically, guardian angels are known for protecting and guarding us in all our activities on earth.

The age-old question always seems to come up right

about now: Why do people get killed if they have guardian angels to protect them? My two thoughts on this subject are that death is not a punishment and that there are certain things we are destined to experience. I don't believe destiny is set in stone, but if we look beyond the event or tragedy and our sense that the angels have abandoned us, eventually we come to understand the spiritual message. This is one of those questions that we simply have to live with. Any answer we come up with is just not going to seem satisfying for very long.

You can ask your guardian angel for knowledge and insight about confusing situations in your life. You can also ask your guardian angel to speak to the guardian angels of people in your life concerning your relationships or interactions with them. Pay attention to your intuition; it will become more brilliant when you are in harmony with your guardian angel, for it is through the inner knowing of intuition that you receive messages from your guardian angel to warn and guide you. Have you ever stopped yourself from doing something because you suddenly had a strong sense it would be a mistake, only to find out later that if you had followed through it would have been disastrous?

Be creative with your guardian angel. In private, be like a child who has an invisible friend and confidant. Guardian angels enjoy this. Children often see and talk to their guardian angels. This usually happens before children can communicate exactly what they see, but some of us can remember far enough back in our lives to a time when we spoke with and saw our guardian angels. If you have children, study their behavior when they are alone. Many children have invisible friends they talk to wherever they are, and babies sometimes seem to stare at someone who isn't there. When babies giggle and grin while sleeping, some say that they are playing with the angels. It is also fun to ask children what they think angels are and to have them draw angels.

In Catholic grade school, children are taught about their guardian angels in first grade. They are taught that their guardian angels are faithful friends who help them while they are on earth by giving them messages about what God wants them to do, and who guard them from evil. Each day they recite the Guardian Angel Prayer, which you'll find reproduced at the end of this section.

Always keep in mind that you have a guardian angel who is the same yesterday, today, and tomorrow. Your guardian angel wants to remind you at this very moment that you are alive, and that whether or not you are happy about this fact, it is true. Your biological and mental "machine" is running on some level of efficiency, and your guardian angel wants to keep you from feeling like a victim. Your guardian angel is looking out for you, waiting to guide you toward your next higher step — whether it is from misery to normalcy, from normalcy to feeling good, or from feeling good to total happiness and delight. Your guardian angel is always by your side, waiting to remind you of the important and special part you play on this crowded planet.

Reciting the Guardian Angel Prayer can help you focus on your guardian angel's presence.

> *Angel of God, my guardian dear,*
> *To whom His love commits me here;*
> *Ever this day [or night], be at my side,*
> *To light and guard, to rule and guide.*

The Halo of Spiritual Guide

When the pupil is ready, the teacher appears.

Spiritual guides come in and out of our lives according to need. They usually represent the essence of a particular culture, race, or religion, or they may represent a career or avenue of life. They are teachers.

When a new guide comes to you, you may find yourself with a voracious urge to know all there is to know about a particular culture or religion previously foreign to you. You start buying books, artifacts, incense, music, or clothes that will teach you the essence of this new interest and its spiritual offerings. Soon, people come into your life who are also studying this essence in their own spiritual quests. Whether this process happens suddenly or subtly, it offers an opportunity for growth in a new direction.

Through meditation or other means, you may be able to see your guides. Basically, all you need to do is notice where your interests lie and listen to messages from within. When you discover your guide or guides, you can accelerate the pace of the lessons you are learning as you explore the many possibilities for growth and for guidance.

For example, if one of your spiritual guides is a Native American, you may have visions that put you in touch with Mother Earth, which may bring you greater respect for the planet, which in turn may inspire you to take action in some way.

If your guide is a Zen Buddhist, your lesson may concern losing your ego for a while, developing intuition, and learning to just be. You may even change jobs to something more basic and less mental in order to learn new ways of being.

It may be that one of your guides represents a personality from the past, such as Florence Nightingale. In this case, your guide may portend a time of service and attention to health and nourishment.

If your guide is Celtic, you may find yourself fascinated with fairy faiths, Arthurian legends, kings and queens, harps, and mystics.

Spiritual guides teach us about spiritual values that are unfamiliar to us. Recognizing our guides through the subtle or dramatics shifts we make in our lives will help us understand our inner goals or a particular spiritual quest. Our guides never really leave us, but they may fade so that other guides can come to the fore when there are new lessons to learn. Spiritual guides are angels of basic teachings; they give us new insight and new creativity to bring us into harmony with our higher selves.

The Halo of Soul Guide

Many people have asked me, "Do we become angels when we die, so that we can watch over those we love?" People who have told me about near-death experiences, or who have done guided imagery exercises of their own deaths, say that when they left their bodies deceased relatives and loved ones were there as angels to guide them into another realm. Many of the angel books I've read relate stories about deceased loved ones relaying important messages back to earth.

According to one Tibetan Buddhist idea, each of us is a composite of aspects drawn from bygone and living personages who have influenced us in some way. Upon death, the composite disassembles and is distributed into the universe, especially to loved ones and to those we have influenced. This process leaves the spirit free of its humanness in the other realm, and benefits the humans left behind. If you have loved ones who have died, remember this idea and claim a part of their composite to bless your own life.

Remember, some questions are meant for us to live with, not answer. One of the questions I live with — and don't worry about having a pat answer to — is: Are guardian angels loved ones who have crossed over? What matters most is your experience, and the feeling it leaves you with. The particulars, the definitions, and the rules are less important.

Whatever else you do, take the love you have deep in your soul for your loved ones who have crossed over and ask that this love continue to grow and transform; ask that this love watch over you. Every once in a while, I feel a blast of love coming to me from someone I have loved who has died. This is a very special feeling; it is very close to the feeling I receive from my contact with angels. Very often this feeling gives me insight and inspiration. Unconditional love has no limits— it can pass back and forth through time and space in an instant — so accept the soul guides who come your way with an open heart.

The Halo of Muse

Creativity comes from the spiritual realm, the collective consciousness. And the mind is in a different realm than the molecules of the brain. The brain is a receiver, not a source.

— CANDACE PERT

Muses are creativity ministers who inspire our talents and gifts. We are all capable of creativity of some kind, but often we need to understand that the wellspring of creativity may rest in a world we don't see. Regardless of where our talents lie, there are muses ready to inspire us far beyond the limits we place on our humanness. There are no limits to creativity when we are inspired by angels. Creativity goes beyond talent to genius when humans develop their ability to listen to inspiration.

In Greek mythology, there are nine muses, the daughters of Mnemosyne (Memory), who are part of Apollo's retinue. These nine daughters are the goddesses of inspiration: Clio of history, Melpomene of tragedy, Urania of astronomy, Thalia of comedy, Terpischore of dance, Calliope of epic poetry, Erato of love verse, Euterpe of lyric poems or music, and Polyhymnia of sacred or religious music.

You may notice that there are three muses directly representing poetry, and many past and contemporary poets acknowledge muses as the source of their inspiration. William Blake, an angel and poet, once said, "I am not ashamed, to tell you what ought to be told — that I am under the direction of messengers from heaven, daily and nightly." Blake attributed all artistic genius to angels.

In ancient Rome, it was customary to thank the genius of the house — the *lares* — at every meal; some homes even set a place for this angel. The *lares* was the spirit of the family's founder and the source of the family's creativity; genius was a part of everyday life. The word *genius* comes from the name for an ancient Roman male's guardian spirit. Juno is the name for the female's guardian spirit. At ancient birthday celebrations, the Romans honored the genius spirit, recognizing it as the source of the individual's imagination.

To muse means to meditate and reflect for creative inspiration.

Whenever you need creative insight, muse away. Get in touch with your own creativity ministers, special angels who can speak to you with inspiration for your particular talent in this lifetime. Whether your gift is solving mathematical problems, painting a masterpiece, or composing great music and literature, learn to listen to your inner guidance to transform talent into genius. Please note that the existence of creative muses does not mean that we can't take credit for our artistic and creative achievements. We are the ones clever enough to expand our consciousness to allow their input, and we are the ones who do the actual work. So give yourself credit for being the genius you are.

The Halo of Cheerleader

Several years ago, I found myself wanting to make a major change in my life. While I knew this change would make my life happier, I wasn't sure how the people closest to me would react. I knew that many of them would not be happy about my decision. Making this decision was leading to painful feelings of guilt, until I discovered my personal cheering section.

Coming out of a meditative state, I got the image of tiny cheerleaders cheering my life on, no matter what I decided to do, even if I made a choice no one else supported. These cheerleaders were cheering, "We like who you are" and "You deserve to be happy; go for it!" I then had the courage to go ahead with my deepest desire, and in time everything worked out for the highest good of all concerned.

You, too, have an angelic cheering section for your higher self. These angels cheer with little voices, "Don't give up.... We like who you are.... Everything's going to be okay.... We're proud of you." Some angels cheer almost everything you do. Their main purpose and function is to support your decisions unconditionally without advice. This is nice when you want to make an eccentric or drastic change and other people seem to be holding you back.

Of course, you won't hear your cheerleaders' voices if you are about to do something unkind or destructive. Below the levels of goodness, the cheerleaders are silent.

Quite often, our deepest desires are difficult to follow because we judge ourselves and our position too harshly. We listen to the advice of others instead of to our inner selves. To know and follow our deepest aspirations may require taking a risk or two. If you venture out on the road of your convictions and find yourself feeling alone, remember that your cheering section and your guardian angel are right there with you and that your loneliness is only temporary. Listen closely; your cheering section is sending words of encouragement: "Go, team, go! Take the ball and run.... Don't look back!"

The Halo of Rescuer

Angels of the moment rescue us in various ways. If we are in grave danger of being physically injured, they will do whatever they can to help us (as long as we are not resistant). Angels of the moment sometimes appear as humans. Or they may come in full angel regalia to rescue someone from the throes of death. Occasionally, we become our higher selves (or our guardian angels) and act as angels of the moment. At these times, we may not even be aware of what we are doing or of the resounding effect we have on situations around us.

I once overhead a telephone conversation at a Thanksgiving dinner celebration in which a close friend of the family was telling her sister about an angel of the moment. This friend was going through a crisis; her husband was in the hospital suffering from a stroke. To add to the stress of the situation, her husband had to be moved to a hospital in the next state (where we live). This woman was staying with her mother, and each day she was driving the freeway, which she had never done before, to be with her husband.

For a while, she wasn't aware of her husband's true condition. One day when she was feeling quite vulnerable and had driven to the hospital without her mother along for support, the doctors informed her that her husband was dying from cancer in its advanced stages. After hearing this news, the woman was left alone in a sterile, cold hallway, feeling lost and helpless. Suddenly, a beautiful young man in his twenties appeared and said, "You look like you could use a cup of coffee."

"Boy, could I," she answered. She went with the young man and had coffee. He made her feel better and even told her she reminded him of his mother, which did wonders for her (she is one of the most effective and loving mothers I know). He said that he was one of a group of volunteers at the hospital and would make sure her husband was fed and looked in on when she wasn't there. After her cup of coffee with this exceptional young man, the woman felt a sense of peace and strength, which enabled her to make the drive home without falling apart.

Then I heard her tell her sister that the young man had just disappeared, and she never saw him again. She ended by saying to her sister, "I think he was some kind of angel."

Yes, he was an angel of the moment. Was he a "real" angel who manifested in the body of a young man, or was the young man's higher self simply being utilized in this situation? Well, whoever he was, he was a rescuer, and he gave this friend a sense of peace and well-being of the sort only angels are capable of transmitting.

The Halo of Synchronism Agent

A new spiritual awakening is occurring in human culture, an awakening brought about by a critical mass of individuals who experience their lives as a spiritual unfolding, a journey in which we are led forward by mysterious coincidences.

— JAMES REDFIELD, *THE CELESTINE PROPHECY*

Have you ever thought that there was something more to coincidence than just random chance? Psychologist Carl Jung and physicist Wolfgang Pauli thought so, and they termed this "something more" *synchronicity*. Synchronicity involves the peculiar interdependent relationship of two events whose connection is apparent to the observer but whose relationship cannot be explained by the principles of causality. Such contemporaneous events seem to influence one another in ways for which we do not yet have a scientific explanation.

Jung explored the relationship between objective "chance" events and the subjective "psychic" state of the observer of these events. One of Jung's theories was that the inner and outer worlds are mysteriously connected, so that something happening in the outside world affects what is happening inside the inner world, or vice versa. Most theories of psychic power say that mind exerts influence over matter, or that the mind can sense or predict events that are distant in time or space.

My own view is that angels are the agents of synchronicity. Not only do angels arrange helpful coincidences; they can also use this power to send us messages. One way they communicate with us is through *synchronisms*. A synchronism is a coincidence for which you recognize that strange "something more." Synchronisms are difficult to describe; they need to be experienced and explored personally.

The first step in developing your capacity to experience synchronisms is to attune your awareness of events and symbols that have meaning to you. Obviously, I have an interest in angels, and many of my synchronisms involve songs with the word *angel* in them. Many times I turn on my radio to find that a song with *angel* in the title is playing or that a phrase about angels is being sung at that very moment. There was a music store that I used to go to about once a week. Each time I visited they were playing a different type of music, and each time I walked in I heard a song with the word *angel* in the lyrics.

Another fun set of synchronisms started for me around 1978, when I was working at an answering service. There are probably only a handful of answering services left today thanks to answering machines, voice-mail systems, and cell phones, but at one time they were very important to many businesses. I worked at the answering service with some fun girls; one of them was a psychic and talked about metaphysical theories all day. Anyhow, this was when digital clocks were just becoming common, and we had to use a digital clock as part of the answering service. A friend and I started to say little prayers whenever we saw double digits on the digital clock. After that, I began to have 11:11 synchronisms. If I was already asleep at 11:11, I would wake up and notice the clock at just that moment. If I was driving, I'd look up to see clocks on banks at 11:11. These 11:11 synchronisms went on and on. I'm sure many of you can relate. One night I was telling some friends about this as we were sitting around talking and listening to music by candlelight. The friend whose house we were at had covered the little clock on the stereo because it was too bright. So after telling my 11:11 stories and having my friends react with a bit of skepticism, I walked over to the stereo, took off the paper that was blocking the clock, and found it read 11:11. I even started to get a bit scared when this first happened, and when November 11 came I thought some disaster was going to happen. It didn't.

Now many of us are seeing 444 and taking it as a sign that our guardian angels are looking over us. Just the other day a woman walked into the art gallery where I work, and I heard someone ask her why she had 444 tattooed on her wrist. He was curious because he kept seeing 444 everywhere. She told him that it was his angels sending him a message of love. So numbers are one of the fun ways the angels remind us that they are near.

Synchronisms are personal, and it is up to you to figure out the "something more" — the meaning. This is tricky, because how do we really know what these events mean? Be careful not to get too excited over the details of synchronisms. Don't get to the place where you are making important decisions based on deeper meanings you have read into a particular situation. Basically, I use synchronisms as an indication that I am on the right track, in the right place, for the right lesson, at the right time. The mere appearance of a compelling synchronism may itself be the message, telling you that you are playing a part in a larger pattern controlled by unseen influences.

Synchronisms are fun. I always smile inside and out when I am blessed with one. They make life more interesting and often provide a dose of much-needed humor.

The Halo of Healer

There is more than enough evidence to support the theory that what goes on in our minds profoundly affects what goes on in our bodies. Healing the body can begin with healing the mind, supplying the mind with what it needs to be healthy and happy. Eliminating negative beliefs that detract from health, and replacing them with positive, healing thoughts, also helps the body heal. Today, many people are healing themselves by changing the way they think, by changing their attitudes toward themselves and toward life.

It is interesting to note *The Oxford American Dictionary*'s definition of *to heal*. These are some of the phrases used: to make whole or sound; to bring to an end or conclusion conflicts between people and groups; to settle and reconcile; to free from evil, cleanse and purify; to form healthy flesh again — to unite after being cut or broken. So, in essence, healing involves repairing and making whole after a separation or break in our lives. Healing is the act of cleaning up messes left over from the past.

Angels can serve as healing agents in many ways. They can help us heal ourselves by channeling healing rays from God. They can help us settle our conflicts with other humans. They can relay messages of forgiveness and reconciliation to others in our lives if we are willing to forgive and forget. Even if the people in question are no longer alive, angels can reach them.

You can ask healing angels for insight into the thought patterns that are blocking integration. Ask them to release learned pain and transmute it. All the methods and practices mentioned in this book can be used for healing with angels. Basically, all angels are healers as well as messengers. So all healing practitioners can call upon angels for extra guidance and love.

Since angels are responsible in part for arranging coincidences, they can arrange for you to find the right doctor or healer for your particular condition. They can also rearrange your cells on a microscopic level, with the help of your own imagination. Visualize angels programming your immune system with healing messages and charging it up with energy.

When people get so sick that they are no longer in control of their own healing energy, or if something terrible happens and they end up in a coma before it is their time to die, healing angels are sent down from God to take charge. These healing angels purify the atmosphere around those who are gravely ill and unconscious. In doing this, they provide a barrier against unwanted and sickening influences. Inside the barrier, they purge the atmosphere of negativity, providing pure, clean, comfortable energy. Then the healing rays of love have direct access to those who are ill and suffering. If you know anyone in such a state, help the angels by visualizing a healing force of angels around the person.

Healing angels do not compete with or feel prejudice against hospitals and medical doctors. Each hospital, whether they know it or not, has its own team of guardian angels. Nurses have been known to see angels around people who are recovering from grave illnesses, and doctors are often guided by divine insight. When healers recognize the role of healing angels, these healers are more powerfully effective in what they do.

Balance of the body/mind and the spirit is the basis for healing. This is a simple concept, but it can be difficult to put into practice. So bring in the healing angels to help you.

The Halo of Humor Transformer

Transformation means making a great change. When we ask for spiritual transformation (either consciously or unconsciously), we get it, and we may be surprised at what it entails. When we are striving for the ultimate spiritual change in our lives, tests and lessons follow us wherever we go. The ride along the road of spiritual transformation is not always smooth, so it is important to take along your sense of humor.

The angels of transformation teach one lesson — humor. They teach us that nothing is serious and that laughing at our human selves is freedom. They teach us to laugh instead of complain. Finding humor in life is not that easy; it is much easier to be serious. Every day, we are plagued by seriousness; just turn on the evening news, and I guarantee you will soon find yourself worrying about your safety, your security, your health, your future — the list goes on and on.

Spiritual transformation is a personal choice each step of the way. The angels won't do it for us; we have to do our own spiritual "work." That is, only we can look inside ourselves and become aware of what we want to transform. But the angels can help us by pointing out the humor in any situation. To find the humor in a seemingly humorless situation, such as being stuck in a spiritual dilemma, stop and ask, "Okay, angels, what's so funny about this one?" We can choose a way out of every dilemma, so choose humor and call upon the humor transformers for assistance to see how funny the dilemma really is.

Do you remember the times when you were a child when you were crying because of something that seemed so dreadfully serious and then all of a sudden the desire to cry would leave and you'd want to laugh but you knew that that would blow it with your parents, yet you couldn't help it and burst out laughing anyway? The humor transformers are ready to restore your sense of divine humor and bring you into a state of grace. So when you lose your desire to be serious, let yourself burst out laughing; the state of grace happens in an instant.

The Halo of Miracle Engineer

According to *The Oxford American Dictionary*, a *miracle* is a remarkable and welcome event that seems impossible to explain by means of the known laws of nature. It is therefore attributed to a supernatural agency. Of course, the supernatural agency is God's crew of angels. Miracles come in many sizes and in various ways. There is a popular bumper sticker that reads: "Expect a Miracle." This is good advice for those of us who are becoming aware of angels, for angels are the engineers who organize and manage miracles.

Love is the force behind miracles. When love is converted into pure, unconditional energy, it heals whatever it touches. Miracles teach and perpetuate love. Miracles can transform those who doubt and hate into those who hope and love. Love, in and of itself, is a miracle. When angels choose insufferable human beings for miracles, they are always trying to teach them that they are loved. Think of Scrooge; he denied love every day until those spirits got ahold of him.

Each time we change our thinking from a negative to a positive program, we have brought about a remarkable and welcome event. Life is a miracle all around us, every day. When you make the choice each day to be happy and not worry, realize what a miracle it is to choose the positive. Over time, small miracles add up to large ones. Miracles do happen, and miracles teach love, unconditionally, through God's agency of miracle engineers.

The Halo of Worry Extinguisher

And who of you by worrying and being anxious can add one unit of measure to his stature or to the span of his life?

— MATTHEW 6:27

Angels love to destroy worry and anxiety. To worry is to torment yourself with disturbing thoughts. Worrying means you are harassing yourself with anxiety over what might happen, or over the consequences of what has already happened. Worry muddies the water of your creative nature, because it takes up too much time and energy. Worry defeats its supposed purpose by not giving you the chance to solve the problem that is worrying you. For if you are in a state of worry, the problem will continue to exist, and it will own you.

If you are worrying all the time, you are taking life too seriously. Why stay up nights worrying about a problem when the solution may be available only during dreamtime? It's easy to fall into the trap of worrying. When you find yourself worrying at a time when you would otherwise be happy and peaceful, call on the worry extinguishers. These angels will take care of whatever is causing you worry, reworking every issue for the highest good of all concerned. Also, if you are worrying about a situation you have yet to face, send the worry extinguishers before you to pave the way. Then notice the recurring patterns of how everything works out. If you are running late to an appointment, the other person will be even later — so why fret on the way? "Let go and let the angels," so that you can use your time for happiness and creativity.

If you find yourself facing a worry that you cannot seem to shake, tune in and ask yourself, "Is this really my business? Is it really my worry?" After examining it, give it to the angels to play with and ask that you be updated when and if you are to act upon it. If you have a worry you can't define and you are carrying around a vague uneasy feeling, do the same. Start to tune in to the feeling. Where is it in your body? When you find its place or residence, shower it with light and imagine the worry extinguishers rushing in to claim it.

> *There are very few things in the mind which eat up as much energy as worry. Worry has never done anyone any good, and it is very much worse than mere dissipation of psychic energy, for it substantially curtails the joy and fullness of life.*
>
> — MEHER BABA, WHO GAVE US
> "DON'T WORRY, BE HAPPY"

The Halo of Happiness Trainer

Many years ago I found a story and picture of a father and son who lived on a well-traveled highway somewhere in Illinois and who were called "the wavers" because all they did all day was sit in the front yard of their junk shop and wave and smile at people traveling down the highway. Sam Chapman and his father, Clarence, spent up to twelve hours a day just waving at passersby. Frequent travelers on this road said that it was a welcome treat to have the wavers smile and wave at them; they said that it changed their mood to a much lighter state. What the waving did was wake them up — wake them up to happiness, wake them out of their state of worry and stress over tight time schedules. Just thinking about the wavers makes me happy; I can see their smiling faces in my mind.

When asked about their job, the wavers said that they had to *train* themselves to be happy and to sit in one place and wave at people all day long. We could all use some happiness training, and luckily for us there are flocks of angels whose sole purpose is to train humans in the art and practice of happiness. These angels want to wake us up to happiness, just as the wavers woke up passing motorists. Could it be that the wavers were angels?

Happiness without reason, regardless of the circumstances in your life, gives you an ease of being in the world. This is the ultimate freedom — to experience a state of happiness you can carry with you wherever you are, whatever you are doing, whoever is with you — the freedom to be unconditionally happy. Claiming and accepting happiness is difficult for most of us. There may be several reasons some people can't accept happiness into their being. Quite often, they feel they have to do everything for themselves without any heavenly help. They don't realize that they can "let go and let the angels."

Accepting happiness may require reprogramming or changing the way you think about life, which may involve reevaluating your priorities and beliefs; this is why we need happiness trainers. Happiness trainers help us identify the things we do that keep us from true, unconditional happiness. They make us aware of the reactions we have to situations that take away happiness. To be happy means being in a state of fascination with life, where situations are simply interesting, not necessarily good or bad.

If you find yourself in a serious mood, look up at the sky and visualize all those happiness trainers waving and smiling at you!

The Halo of Fun Executive

Have you ever really thought about fun? *The Oxford American Dictionary* defines *fun* as that which provides lighthearted amusement and enjoyment. When we do something we like, we say, "This is fun." Sometimes, work can become play; if we like it, then it is fun. Wouldn't it be great if everything we did provided lighthearted amusement? Well, that might be taking it a bit too far, but in this day and age we definitely need to bring more fun into our lives. Angels' work is their play. The fun executives are always ready to provide light for your heart in any situation. They get their name from knowing how to manage fun and put it into effect.

When we set aside time for fun, sometimes we don't know what to do. We might go on vacation, expecting to have lots of fun, but instead we become bored. How ironic life can be! Adults often say, "I'm too busy to have fun." Games are supposed to provide fun, and most jobs are like games — there are rules, scores, players, and goals. So why isn't work fun? Work isn't fun because we take it seriously and focus too much on ourselves.

Fun is like happiness; it depends not on circumstances but on our being in synch with ourselves and the universe. Fun is Zen; it requires full, effortless attention to the moment. Once again, children can serve as our teachers. Watching children play can make time stand still; children are right in the moment, letting their imaginations run wild, taking cues from their friends, and creating fun. Children at play scream with glee and laughter. Angels want us to have fun — fun we can take with us to work, to leisure time, to any activity. Angels provide us with light-hearted amusement.

Think of a time that was really fun. It probably came about unexpectedly, with people you never imagined you'd enjoy. Maybe it started out as an adventure, exploring new ground. Maybe you were by yourself, cleaning your house, and it turned out to be fun. Fun is possible anywhere, anytime; it really is. When you are in a situation that isn't fun and you want it to be, take a time-out to get into synch by relaxing into the moment. If you're suffering from boredom, then do something about it. Get out, and ask the angels for a change. Don't grow up; regress if necessary. Find the child within you and learn to play again. Fun is contagious; let it start with you and then spread to those around you.

The Halo of Mirth Maker

Mirth is like a flash of lightning, that breaks through a gloom of clouds, and glitters for a moment; cheerfulness keeps up a kind of daylight in the mind, and fills it with a steady and perpetual serenity.

— JOSEPH ADDISON

Mirth is a little different from fun, although the two often go together. Picture a large, round oak table lighted by many candles. Around the table is a party of friends who are practicing the "eat, drink, and be merry" religion. Joyful music is playing, and the laughter verges on uncontrolled hilarity, exceeding the limits of propriety and reason. Everything is amusing and thus provides an excuse to laugh and giggle. Glee, the effervescence of high spirits and ecstatic gestures, is alive at this table. Good nature, good spirits, benevolent joviality, and a sense of love for all hold reign as the sights and sounds of merriment continue. When added together, joy, merriment, glee, laughter, and fun equal mirth.

Mirth goes a step beyond fun. Mirth is like a magic spell cast over those participating in fun. It involves the merriment of the moment, not necessarily wit and fun making. You may find the example of mirth given in the above paragraph a bit too gustatory for a book on angels, but angels understand that we are humans and that we need to eat and drink together. Angels appreciate the sense of communion we experience when we share meals with others. Mirth is meant to be shared, and angels create it to share with us. If we could see the angels at the party described, they would be dancing, giggling, and singing with joy right in the midst of all the human activity.

Of course, we don't have to be eating to be graced with mirth. Being in love or taking a long walk with the one you love can be quite mirthful. Actually, anything you do when you are in love with life can be mirthful.

It would be difficult to have mirth without the angels; it is their invention. If you need mirth in your life for you and those you love, ask the mirth makers. Mirth makers are always ready to celebrate by adding extra joy and laughter to happiness. You may need to be the instigator, so follow your heart to the gleeful side of life, to mirth.

The Halo of Prosperity Broker

Prosperity is the art of being financially successful and fortunate. Prosperity doesn't mean having hoards of money; it means that the money you have is managed in a positive way. Regardless of what we have on paper, it's the way we live that makes us prosperous. Money is like energy: If it is used, it creates more; if it is stifled and stored, it absorbs you. To use money as energy, we cannot be attached to it. We are wise to release money with the positive thought that it will continue to work for us, that the energy cycle will not be broken. If you want freedom but you work all day with the belief that only money will give it to you, when will you ever have the time to be free?

Money is an apparition, a dream; if you chase after it as if it were real, you become part of a dream, different from what you are. This dream can become a nightmare and cause a person extreme detriment and desperation. The belief that having money is good and not having money is bad is limiting and mistaken; having money is totally useless unless you have a use for it, and if the use you have in mind is a negative one, then money can be destructive. By the same token, not having money is a problem only at those crucial moments when you need money. Prosperity brokers can help move those crucial moments around to the times when you have money — hence, no problem.

Call in the prosperity brokers to teach you the true essence of wealth and abundance. Wealth and abundance come from an attitude of seeing our lives as fortunes in and of themselves, rich and plentiful with enough to go around. With a prosperous attitude comes a knowing that the universe will take care of us. The prosperity brokers make invisible deals for you, which may involve transferring your wealth — that is, converting time, energy, and ideas into more negotiable commodities. Or they may make deals to enable you to enjoy your wealth more with love. Or they may need to teach you about gratitude — to be grateful for what you do have rather than focus on scarcity. They may teach you to be grateful for each moment as a precious gift and thankful for each situation as a valuable lesson regardless of what you have in your wallet.

The Halo of Nature Guardian or Deva

The devic kingdom is the perpetuating life force of nature. It has a hierarchy of its own. Devas are the royalty of nature; they hold the archetypal patterns of every species on earth. Devas oversee entire landscapes. The smaller nature spirits, such as fairies, elves, gnomes, wood sprites, nymphs, and fauns, are given the blueprints of various plant forms, and they become the craftspeople who tend to the smallest details of each plant. In a sense, what angels are to human beings, these little spirits are to plants and animals — sources of guidance and perfection.

The devic kingdom wants to share nature with us in a harmonic way, bringing us joy through the glorious creations of flowers, trees, fields of wheat, tropical forests, and so forth.

The devic kingdom helps teach us respect for the earth and its energy currents.

Have you ever been inside a building that didn't feel right for some reason? Outside, the landscape held a barren, empty feeling in places, and the plants didn't seem to grow very well despite ample watering and care. On the other hand, maybe you have noticed how some houses seem to fit right into the natural setting of the land; the plant life around them is lush, and the ambiance feels "right." Or maybe you have a favorite park with these characteristics. The Chinese have a word for this subtlety: *feng shui* (which, translated literally, means "wind-water"). When the *feng shui* is right, there is an alignment with the wavelike *chi* currents of the earth. In the West, this understanding is referred to as *geomancy*, which is based on the premise that humans do not act upon the earth; they interact with it.

The devas can help you get the *feng shui* right in your own environment by sending you messages concerning exactly where to build and plant and how to landscape. As always, the best way to receive messages from the devas or from any angel is to pay quiet attention to your intuition. If you are planting a garden, take your time to find the right spot for it by listening to nature. Open your heart and mind to the devic kingdom, and the devas will give you creative ideas for the *feng shui* of your place in the universe.

For more information about the devic kingdom, read Dorothy Maclean's *To Hear the Angels Sing*. This inspiring book relates messages Dorothy received from the devas on how to grow the miracle garden at Findhorn (the website for Findhorn Garden is included in the Resources section at the back of this book).

Designing a Personal Halo

There may be some areas in your life that the angels described so far don't seem to fit. Well, no problem! You can simply ask that an angel suited to this area take over. Basically, all you have to do is define the situation and name the angel who is supposed to take charge of it. A custom-designed angel will arrive and take on the job. In this way, you can draw to you your own personal flock of angels.

Designer angels can help with a variety of situations. For example, if you are a teacher, you may want to name an angel of education to watch over and guide you. You might name the angel something like Socrates or Horace. If you are a student, you can call upon a designer angel to help you study.

If you are a writer, call in a specific angel to help you write. Give the angel an appropriate name, maybe the name of a character in your next bestseller. Also, it is always helpful to get in touch with the angel of the typewriter or word processor you use when you are writing; this angel can help you in a variety of ways.

You can also call upon designer angels for help with the communication arts or communication in general. Send angels with the letters you write, the emails you send, and the phone calls you make.

If you're an artist, you can get very specific and name angels for your paints and for certain colors you are using; you can even assign angels to your favorite paintbrush and to each masterpiece you create.

If you are a businessperson, assign an angel of profit and an angel of customer increase or customer service to your business.

Think of your hobbies and the way you spend most of

your time. There's room for angels in every activity and in every moment of the day. Some angels like to cook, even though they can't eat what they create!

Assign an angel to be the guardian of your hearth and home — to create a loving atmosphere where peace prevails. You can even assign an angel to each room. Set a place at the dinner table for your home guardian and designate a place where this angel can sit in your living room.

Angels are always ready to assist in the process of birth, especially in the birth of human beings. Angels like to be included in the miracle of creation from the very beginning. Invite them in. Of course, your guardians will be there anyway, but they enjoy company.

Angels can be assigned to groups or organizations. Any group with an enlightened cause, whether it be promoting healthy fun for the individuals in the group or working toward world peace, has a group mind. If you belong to a group fitting these criteria, then acknowledge the group angel. The group angel represents the group mind. You can regard the group angel as the guardian of the group, and you can send this angel before you. Also, be sure to ask the group angel to guide you into the group mind to work out problems and create new awareness.

Keep in mind that designing angels is a fun and creative activity; it is not meant as a way to manipulate the world around us. That would not be in alignment with the spirit of angel consciousness. The angels are always pointing us to the Divine. Whatever our mission in life, it is best to relax and take our time. Instead of looking for ways to "get ahead," it is more important to pay attention to doing our best right now. The angels, no matter what halos they are wearing, are always standing by, willing and able to help us do just that.

CHAPTER TWO

Angel Consciousness

> *The deeper the self-realization of a man, the more he influ-*
> *ences the whole universe by his subtle spiritual vibrations,*
> *and the less he himself is affected by the phenomenal flux.*
>
> — P. YOGANANDA'S MASTER

*A*ngels act as messengers of God. They communicate with us through inspiration. When we fill our everyday lives with spiritual essence and ask the angels to join us, we create angel consciousness. Angel consciousness entails more than just focusing on the wonder of angels; its scope includes notic-ing the wonder of God everywhere and in everything, and sharing and cocreating this wonder with the angels. Angel con-sciousness helps us keep heavenly qualities alive right here on earth. We not only *see* the beauty around us; we *feel* it in our souls. We don't merely *hear* celestial music; our beings *resonate* to it. Angels, as messengers of heaven, help us make life a true and meaningful experience. This in turn allows us to raise the vibration of love on planet earth. If you want to be a part of expanding the light of love on earth right now, a good and a fun way to start is by filling your consciousness with angels.

> *Consciousness: the state of being awake and aware of what is*
> *going on around you; somebody's mind and thoughts; the set*
> *of opinions, feelings, and beliefs of a group; awareness of or*
> *sensitivity to issues in a particular field; the part of the human*
> *mind that is aware of the feelings, thoughts, and surroundings.*
>
> — ADAPTED FROM *THE AMERICAN HERITAGE DICTIONARY*

Often when people first start to increase their angel con-sciousness, their whole perception of life changes. People feel very happy when they find out that they can focus on something that is solely positive in nature. When we bring angel consciousness into our everyday lives, we experience real shifts. We notice that a force bigger than us is at play in our lives for the highest good of all. We see, sense, hear, feel, know, and enjoy positive results.

Once you develop angel consciousness, you won't have to *believe* in angels, because you will *know* them. You will be experiencing life with them. When you enter into angel consciousness, there is no separation between an angel experience and a personal experience. Angel consciousness means you know that you are a divine being and that you are guided by a higher wisdom in the universe that operates for your highest good. Angel consciousness points us toward the truth that life is meant to be enjoyed and lived, not suffered and endured.

Something changes in us when we become aware of the love and guidance always available from the angels. This is not a fad, or a trend, or a passing fancy; angel consciousness is a way of life. Many people wonder why the angels are so popular with the masses right now. Some people think that there is so much darkness on earth that the angels are making themselves known to correct this. Others feel we are on the verge of a total enlightening of the planet. My inner knowing tells me that God is in process, and I am not about to second-guess God. I trust the bigger picture behind all of this. I feel that the angels are so prevalent in people's lives right now to keep the beautiful aspects of being human from becoming extinct and to encourage us to be the magnificent creatures we are meant to be. The angels want us to keep our hearts in the right place and feed the world's soul with the arts of love, laughter, grace, and our natural creative energy. Regardless of how technologically organized the world may become, if we don't keep love and laughter alive, there will be nothing left to nourish our spirits.

Angels and Our Physical Senses

Remember, most of us do not see angels as physical objects. Some have seen angels as fields of dazzling light, too bright to stare at for long. If you do see an angel, the angel will probably take a form you are willing to accept. Most of us have seen pictures of angels with wings and halos. If you want to imagine angels as beautiful humans with wings, this is fine; if an angel is destined to appear to you, he or she will probably oblige you by taking such a form. Angels have appeared to people throughout history, but this is rare and generally surrounds a "big event."

To get to know angels, it helps if you can transcend the "seeing is believing" paradigm and adopt an open mind and a stance of "knowing by intuition." Reality is much more than just what we see. And it is much more than what we hear. Consider for a moment the field of electromagnetic energy that surrounds us; we know this field exists, but we cannot see or hear it with our usual physical senses. We need some kind of receiver. For example, radio and television signals are silent and invisible to us until we turn on a radio or a television set, but these signals exist around us all the time. We see physical objects through their reflection of a narrow band of the frequencies called "visible light," but we see only the rays of light that actually enter the pupils of our eyes, not the entire three-dimensional field of electromagnetic "light" energy that surrounds us.

Candace Pert is one of the scientists who discovered endorphins. Endorphins are natural opiates found in our brains that act as filtering mechanisms. They function by selectively filtering the incoming information from every sense (sight, hearing, smell, taste, and touch), including pain, blocking some of it from percolating up to higher levels of consciousness. As Candace Pert states, "Each organism has evolved so as to be able to detect the electromagnetic energy that will be most useful for its survival. Each has its own *window on reality*." The British writer and thinker Aldous Huxley spoke of the nervous system and the brain being like a "reducing valve" or filter that enables us to experience only a fraction of reality.

If every sense is selectively filtering environmental information, and if some of what is happening around us is not being registered by our usual waking consciousness, then consider this: Part of the reality that we are filtering out is angelic activity. Angels are very busy, and they exist in many places at once; if we could see them readily, we would experience chaos, and we might all go crazy. When saints and mystics hear voices and see visions, other people get frightened and tend to label them insane.

Legend has it that in ancient times angels, fairies, elves, brownies, and various other magical creatures were easy to see and talk to (perhaps this is the origin of folklore and fairy tales). Anyway, humans became so preoccupied with the magic of this realm that they were not paying attention to the physical world. So for the sake of their growth and survival, humans for the most part had to turn off the ability to see and hear these magical creatures. I have talked to several people who do "see" angels, but they don't like to talk or boast about it, because it is very personal and sacred.

When we "hear" angels, we may hear a beautiful chorus of voices singing in the distance. I have heard about angels embellishing the music we are listening to with their singing (if they like it). Or we may hear sweet tingling bells or chimes at subtle times when angels are around us.

Angels sometimes leave a fragrant scent, without a recognizable source, for us to smell in unexpected places. They especially like the floral scents of rose and jasmine.

Some people know angels are with them because at strategic moments they feel hands touch them gently upon their shoulders, or they feel a presence so strong it compels them to look around for someone who isn't there.

Don't worry if you don't have magical, imaginal, or physical sensations regarding angels. Angels are not here to interfere with our growth, and some of us get carried away with magical thinking and mystical experiences. The most important attitudes to cultivate in attracting angels are optimism, unconditional love, and happiness. Angels surround people who are truly happy and loving, encouraging more love and happiness. Whether you can experience them readily with your physical senses is unimportant. What matters is finding a way to know angels for yourself, and steering clear of the "seeing is believing" nonsense we have all heard at one time or another.

Angels are like thoughts. We cannot see our thoughts, but we know they exist. We can have as many thoughts as we want; there is no limit. Imagine for a moment a source field where thoughts become form. Think of a positive, loving thought as a blessing. Imagine how it travels as a healing beam of light to whomever the thought was about. See it reach the person and lighten up his or her heart and mind. Now that person has a light heart and sends out blessings. The original blessing has created a chain reaction of happiness that reaches out to more and more people. Now imagine what a negative thought can do. I won't describe each link in this chain, but I'm sure your imagination will help you see the damage negative thoughts can do.

Thoughts are powerful and real even though we don't see them — and so are angels. All of us have our "own window on reality," so we experience angels in our own ways. There is, however, a common denominator: Angels don't hurt us; they help us. Messages, experiences, happenings, thoughts, and feelings that interfere with or limit our well-being and separate us further from our higher selves do not originate from angels. Angels exist in a realm of positive, loving energy and pink love light. When we have peak experiences of joy and love, we have connected with the angels. Angels don't have peak experiences; they *are* peak experiences. (Angels don't experience the ups and downs we humans do.) Angels serve as models of the joyful and happy thoughts we can share.

To have angels in our lives, we need to welcome them by cultivating and practicing the things that angels vibrate in harmony with. To allow the angels to dance in our consciousness, we need to create a dance floor where they can express themselves fully. The angels vibrate at a very high level, and they can't help further vibrations of a low nature, such as greedy intentions. Beauty, prayer, gracious offerings, and simplicity, when practiced with a loving heart, allow us direct cocreative energy with the angels. Once we pass through the phase of amazement regarding angels and let go of focusing on their awesome powers, we arrive at the ultimate stage of angel consciousness, where we make the choice to use our free will and gift of life to love God and help the angels bring forth and preserve the beautiful qualities of life.

A theory is something we use to help us understand phenomena. Theories don't need to be tested to be useful; we can simply use theories as a way to study and think. Often in this book I share one of my theories and hope that you will either use the information to create your own theory or discard it if it doesn't fit your theory. One theory I like to think about is that when we vibrate high enough and radiate enough light and love, then we become almost invisible to forms of life that are vibrating at lower rates. This can be a saving grace at times, and we may not know when it occurs. Angels vibrate to Divine Love, which is the highest vibration in the universe, the highest light wave out there. This is why we don't readily see angels with our eyes; they are vibrating above the physical spectrum of light. God is the ultimate source of all light and love. We cannot drain this source. When we take from Divine Love, there is more love created for all concerned. When we choose to be vibrant with love, we replenish and energize the world around us with light.

Initiating an Angelic Mind-set

Keep walking, though there is no place to get to.
Don't try to see through the distances.
That's not for human beings.
Move within, but don't move the way fear makes you move.

— RUMI

To be amusing I used to say, "A mind is a terrible thing." I didn't really mean it, but at times it almost seems true. Because we play in the fields of the mind when we read, I want to help you form a mind-set that allows full openness to the angels, one that will help keep your mind from being a terrible thing. First we will explore the wonderful world of faith.

Having faith means we believe or have a "knowing" about something without having logical proof. Faith takes us past "shoulds" to a sense that everything is perfect in being what it is. Faith is our grounding wire for a spiritual mind-set.

A *mantra* is a sacred word, chant, or sound we repeat to facilitate spiritual power and transformation of consciousness. "Faith, not fear" is an especially powerful mantra. Use this mantra often; repeat it whenever you feel disconnected or unsure. When worry and anxiety creep into my consciousness with negative messages, I stop and repeat, "Faith, not fear." This changes my chemistry, and the essence of the angels begins to brighten my consciousness. Each time I wonder how I'm going to pay the rent or what I'm going to do about such and such, I stop and begin to repeat, "Faith, not fear." Then I remember that with God all things are possible. As I repeat this mantra, I relax my shoulders and focus on releasing neck tension. I tune into any areas in my body that need to let go of negative energy. Then I take a few deep breaths and imagine angelic light filling my being. I energize the intent of "being here now." Some days I find myself repeating the mantra throughout the day; other days one dose is all I need.

You may wonder why this mantra acknowledges fear. Adding the word *fear* gives us the chance to recognize what takes us away from our spiritual center. We can't deny fear in our lives. Some fears help to protect us, but the fears that cripple us live in our minds. As Gavin de Becker states in *The Gift of Fear*: "Like every creature, you can know when you are in the presence of danger. You have the gift of a brilliant internal guardian that stands ready to warn you of hazards and guide you through risky situations. By trusting your 'gut feeling,' rather than logic, you can be more grounded in nature and make smarter choices. Fear is a signal in the presence of danger, but unwarranted fear or anxiety is always based on your memory or imagination."

Good Questions

Byron Katie is an interesting spiritual teacher I happened upon a few years ago. She teaches what she calls "The Work." One of the basic premises consists of asking yourself four questions. I find these questions to be a great tool for changing the chemistry of a fearful or stuck mind-set, such as ruminating endlessly over something. The four questions are:

1. Is it true?

2. Can I absolutely know that it's true?

3. How do I react when I think that thought?

4. Who would I be without the thought?

I also appreciate the part of The Work where Katie says: "There are only three kinds of business: my business, your business and God's business. When a thought passes through the mind, ask yourself: 'Whose business am I in with this thought?'"

I like The Work because it helps us tune into what might be jamming our frequency in the moment; by focusing our awareness, we create the change we seek. As always, ask the angels to help with this work. They will start the changes on the inner planes as we work on the outer levels.

Faith in the Ultimate Wisdom of the Universe

Experiencing complete trust in God and the angels is not always easy. An ancient story that has been told many ways illustrates this dilemma. The version I like best tells of Moses and the Green One.

Moses meets the Green One in the desert, and they begin to travel together. The Green One tells Moses that he has some deeds to do, and he fears Moses will not be able to witness these deeds without judging them with indignation. He tells Moses that if he cannot trust and bear with him, he will have to leave.

Moses agrees to this, as he does not want the Green One to leave because he feels that he is in the presence of a great teacher. Eventually, Moses and the Green One come upon a fishing village, where the Green One begins to sink all the fishing boats of the villagers. Moses is quite upset by this, but he remembers his agreement not to judge and he says nothing.

Next, they arrive at the decaying house of two devoted young men who live just outside the wall of a city of nonbelievers. The Green One goes up to the wall, which is falling down, and repairs it, but he ignores the house of the two believers. Again Moses is disturbed and confused, but he keeps quiet.

They continue traveling, and the Green One keeps doing things that upset Moses. Finally Moses witnesses something so intolerable that he can no longer refrain from making a comment and interpreting the situation. The Green One now has to leave him, but before he goes he tells Moses why he acted as he did. With regard to the sunken fishing boats, the Green One tells Moses that pirates were on the way to steal the boats; by sinking them, he saved the boats from being stolen. As for the two believers, the Green One fixed the wall of the non-believers to save the two believers from ruin; their life's fortune was buried under the city wall and was about to be revealed and stolen. The Green One leaves, and Moses realizes that all he had judged as bad and intolerable was in fact neither.

I think this story describes our walk with the angels. To walk with the angels, we are called on to be awake and aware. This means we may witness many things we can't believe God would allow. God doesn't explain them to us the way the Green One finally explained things to Moses, so we have to keep trusting at times when we are about to lose faith. Essentially the story illustrates how often we second-guess God and the angels, or label something bad before we understand the whole picture.

Projecting Vibrations

Last summer before I had the chance to actually see the movie *What the #$BLEEP*! Do We Know!?* — a movie I highly recommend everyone see — I went to the website and discovered Masaru Emoto's work, which is featured in a scene from the movie (see the Resources section at the back of this book for website addresses for both the movie and Masaru Emoto). Then I bought Emoto's book *The Hidden Messages in Water*.

In a series of experiments, Emoto directed specific, concentrated thoughts toward water while it froze into ice crystals. In his book is a photograph of the words *love* and *gratitude* shown to water as it froze. The photo depicts a perfect crystal radiating golden light; it touches your soul. Emoto says that this "indicates that love and gratitude are fundamental to the phenomenon of life in all of nature." Water subjected to words such as "You make me sick" looks sick and shows no crystals; instead, it looks polluted. So, if you were thinking that negative feelings and beliefs are fairly harmless, think again.

Another key truth that Masaru Emoto points out in his book is that "existence is vibration," that "each thing generates its own frequency, which is unique." Angels vibrate at a high frequency. This is not a judgment call; it is just what is. The angels respond to our vibrational level and interact with us accordingly. They respond instead of judge.

In figuring out what exactly negative emotions are, it's important to remember that sadness and grief are not negative in nature. We may not enjoy responding with deep emotion and it may not always be comfortable, but it is real and comes from our hearts. Let's also consider how we change all day when we are living authentically. If a wave of grief passes over us, we may have the urge to cry. The next moment could bring a perception of humor that leaves us laughing. This is healthy, not crazy.

There are times when my heart breaks for the world, and I feel deep grief. I don't feel I am projecting negativity when these feelings come to me, or that I am getting stuck in a fearful scenario. Sadness has a form of beauty all of its own. The important thing is that we start to identify our mind-set and vibrational level. This will be unique to us, and the angels will teach us along the way. Happiness is a vibration mixed with authenticity, not superficial, forced peppiness.

It's also important to be aware of how we actually *behave* in response to our feelings or thoughts. If I am feeling hatred, I have choices about how to deal with it. If I behave hatefully, then I will cause damage; if I look inside to find where my hatred is originating and work on changing it, no outward damage has been done. This principle also works the other way around. If I feel love but do nothing about it in the way I behave, then no loving actions have taken place.

Constructive Vibrations

As humans we have many energy patterns, guides, or archetypes that shepherd us in experiencing life. We interact with energy in many different ways. Some of these involve the following: rhythm, systems, instinct, will, impulse, attitude, connection, response, radiation, affirmations, attunement, alignment, comfort, and resonance.

Constructive vibrations are important for our work with affirmations, healing, and intention. First of all, consider the obvious. For example, using "kill energy" to "right wrongs" and attempt to reset balance is not a way to attract angels. Part of our societal thinking cries out for us to kill pain, kill murderers, kill enemies, kill thoughts, and kill cancer cells. Using kill energy, such as imagining cancer cells being destroyed, may not be the best way to alter our chemistry or bring healing. People studying the effects of thought and prayer on cells have found that loving energy sends a message to return to balance, whereas kill energy may simply upset our internal balance. Balance and wholeness are the keys to healing.

Much too often in our quest for personal power, we let our egos guide the way. We don't stop to look at all the particulars residing within the outcomes we are putting energy toward. We need to embody the golden rule if we are to receive help from the angels. So when you are looking to create positive change, consider the whole picture. Put yourself in the place of all the people involved and ask yourself whether you would want that if you were them. Sincerely look at the effect your actions could have on the world around you. Does your quest involve competition, taking advantage of others, or a hidden agenda?

Inviting the Angels In

When we invite the angels to help us in our day-to-day lives, we are apt to experience an immediate transcendental shift in consciousness. The angels play behind the scenes, in ways we wouldn't think of, to help us put into action our heartfelt dreams.

Everyone receives guidance from the angels; some are simply more aware of it than others. Angels often come into our lives suddenly and unexpectedly, altering our perceptions so that when they leave, the changes in our consciousness remain, even if our experience of them is hidden in our unconscious, like a dream we know we had but can't quite remember. This kind of angelic presence is a theme in countless movies, where angels come down to earth in human form to help people in crisis, and then disappear once their mission is accomplished, leaving behind only the vaguest sensation of a mystical presence. Those who have had a bona fide transformation of consciousness with the angels will continue to receive heavenly grace, blessings, and hope in their darkest hours — and a divine sense of humor to make their lives soar with love, light, and laughter.

Angel consciousness and peace consciousness go hand in hand. When we have angel consciousness, we know that we are divine beings, guided by a higher wisdom that operates for our highest good. This trust in a higher wisdom is essential to a peaceful outlook. We can truly say we know peace when we are able to accept and adapt to all changes that might occur in our lives, maintaining a sense of confidence in a higher good no matter what befalls us.

Inspiration in the Air

The world of thought resides in the air. All of our thoughts happen in the air element. Our greatest thoughts come to us from the generosity of the air. It is here that the idea of inspiration is rooted — you inspire or breathe in the thought concealed in the air element.

— JOHN O'DONOHUE

Air is the link between earth and heaven, between our physical and spiritual selves. We tend to think that air is empty and idle since it's something that we don't typically see in the same way that we see a fire or a waterfall. Take a moment and think about all of the things happening in the air right now. How does it feel: warm, cool, damp, dry? What does it smell like? If you are inside a dwelling, think about the difference in the air outside. Think about all the signals passing through the air right now. Think about where the angels are. When my friend Shannon's son

Gideon was around six years old, we asked him what he thought angels were, and he answered, "Oh, they are just plain old air."

We experience air in continually changing ways. Air may be still and calm, or heavy with impending rain. It may be warm with the comfort of the summer, or chilly with the breath of winter. It may come with the sweet touch of a gentle breeze or the fury of a tornado. It may carry us along on a strong wind, within which there may be other winds — forces of energy and change blowing simultaneously, taking part of us here and part of us there, or masking inner movement with an outward appearance of stillness.

The air is the realm of ideas, and air reminds us of the power of ideas. As thought always precedes action, so success in any endeavor is best built on a firm strategic foundation, with divine inspiration to energize it. Inspiration is the breath of God. It is the divine life force that keeps us vital. The best thing about inspiration is that it is free. You cannot actually buy it, even though it may come from something you bought. Inspiration exists within and around you at all times; your job is to clean out your inspiration receptor sites.

Too much talk and explanation can drive away the special energy and gift of inspiration. For example, say you read a beautiful story about the experience of someone who witnessed a true happening from heaven, and it leaves your skin tingling and a feeling of hope in your heart. Consider what happens when you start thinking too much about it and asking questions that only God can answer, such as "Why did the angels guide this person out of sickness or danger, and let others suffer or die in similar instances? How do we know this really happened, and the person isn't just making up a story?" Inspiration is a gift to the mind, yet the mind can easily block it or ruin it.

I have noticed over the years that writers and scholars who need to be known for their intellects but want to write about angels tend to get overly technical about issues such as whether angels have wings. In fact, I have read books that seem to be trying to wipe out popular conceptions of angels, replacing beautiful imaginings with dull recitations. I wonder where these writers and scholars are getting their information. Is it from deep knowing and experience? And if so, of what?

As humans we respond to symbols. We express divine insights in our art. If there is a preponderance of art depicting angels with wings, obviously this symbolizes something real within the collective psyche. The angelic experience is a connection with divine beauty. Angels appear to humans in a particular form so that they will be able to accept and understand the appearance. Wings are symbolic of a divine connection, so let it be. Since when did arguing over the particulars of angels — such as how many dance on the head of a pin and so forth — give us anything but a headache?

As we learn how to use inspiration, we open new vistas that lead to creative thinking and expression. We are able to think freely because we aren't looking for absolutes all the time. Instead, we are inspired to follow love, which doesn't tend to follow a straight line.

Imagination

Imagination is more important than knowledge.

— ALBERT EINSTEIN

Imagination is the art and practice of producing ideal creations, forming clear mental images, and creating feelings.

Your imagination is your future. It is the only place the future exists. When you want something, it's important to be able to visualize it and produce an ideal image of it in your mind. When you use your imagination with faith, you know without effort what you want and how to attain it because you already have it in your mind. Allowing the feeling to emerge helps to manifest what we want in the physical realm. Imagination is your direct connection to the angels.

With faith, imagination, the angels, and God, you can do anything. If you are having trouble experiencing angels, use your imagination and faith to get to know their ways. Imagine everything you can about angels — what you already know and what you want to know. Imagine meeting an angel; imagine what the angel would look like, what you would talk about, and what the angel would sound like, smell like, and feel like. Visualize floating into the etheric realm and flying with the angels through all the heavenly colors. If you aren't having much luck with this, keep trying!

While the rational, logical part of society discounts flights of imagination as unreal, in fact the imagination is our direct line to true intelligence and greatness. The great inventions of the world are conceived in the womb of imagination, as are the great works of art. It is through our imaginations that we connect with the future and meet the angels in their purest form. When we are in an imaginative state, we are completely open to all sorts of possibilities, and highly receptive to angelic guidance. And that guidance, if followed, tends to turn imaginings into happenings. Your most impossible dreams are, indeed, all in your imagination — just waiting to become reality.

The imagination, then, is a profound reality. It is not a

place that we create through fantasy, a world that we simply "make up." The imagination is actually the operating room of the soul, the place where we connect to our deepest and highest selves. Why else would Albert Einstein have declared, "Imagination is more important than knowledge"? Einstein, after all, was one of the supreme examples of someone who understood that a meaning and truth exist above and beyond the limits of our logical, practical minds. Because he was given to daydreaming and allowed images to speak to him, Einstein was able to transcend physical reality and formulate his astounding theory of relativity. He respected the imagination as the birthplace of creativity — in his case, the kind of creativity that would alter society's perception of the entire universe.

The unconscious is as valid a region as the conscious, and even more valid, for it directs us through life and can make things quite uncomfortable for us when we ignore its messages, pleas, and warnings. The imagination is the meeting place of our conscious and unconscious, the place where the potter's wheel of the mind fashions a work of art from the clay of the soul.

Subatomic Particles

I found the following article on subatomic particles on the Internet, and I realized that all the descriptions of subatomic particles fit the angels too. Owen Waters, editor of InfiniteBeing.com, gave me permission to share it here (information about this website is included in the Resources section at the back of this book).

If you believe that you exist in a fixed location in space and that time must always pass you by like clockwork, think again. Subatomic particles do not share your beliefs about time and space. They take a much more liberated view. Subatomic particles pop in and out of physical manifestation millions of times per second, just when and where they feel like it. Their disregard for time is perplexing, to say the least, as they respond immediately to events in their future and even time travel backwards to alter their past when it suits them.

Now, we can all identify with the idea of creating a different future based on decisions that we make now, but creating a different past? Well, that's what subatomic particles do, right there in the lab. As a result, in the mathematics of quantum physics today, one of the necessary tools is negative time — the ability of a particle to send a message into its past in order to change its own history.

Subatomic particles are friendly by nature. When they bump into another particle that they take a liking to, and they seem to like all of them, they become friends and carry on communicating with each other, forever. The fact that they may become separated by millions of miles does not reduce their willingness to communicate.

The speed of their communications comes as a surprise. Einstein said that nothing exceeds the speed of light, but apparently subatomic particles weren't listening when he said that. They communicate over huge distances virtually instantly. If there is a limit to the speed of transmitted thought, then that speed of thought has to be millions of times faster than the speed of light.

Subatomic particles, by their very freedom, serve to remind us of our true potential as conscious beings in a conscious universe. We are limited only by our personal collection of beliefs, our belief system. We also share our part of a larger, societal belief system, the consensus reality.

As an Angel

Imagine for a moment that you are an angel assigned to watch over humans. You are a being of pure light and spirit; you can be wherever you need to be quicker than an instant. You do all you do for the Great Creator of Love, and for the heavens. You are a curator of divine beauty, grace, and enlightenment. You have spent eternity watching humans. You have witnessed all the missed opportunities for love. You have seen humans blessed with everything needed to bring them delight and happiness, and yet you've watched them continually suffer through life. You have witnessed and most likely helped deep moments transpire when humans became truly divine. You have seen hearts open in these profound moments, when love is imprinted on the world in ways beyond human imagination.

As an angel you may have been a bit envious of the way humans can *physically* create love, beauty, and life itself. Humans can reach out and hug loved ones in a warm exchange of sweetness. Humans can be physically present for one another in moments of compassion, when great healing takes place. This is perhaps something you have witnessed and helped to come about many times as an angel but have never been able to experience in physical form.

You have seen how happy God is with humans who make love the guiding purpose of their lives, so you have taken the leap of faith and asked God to be born a human. Now as a human you are more than ready to go out and create love. As an angel now human, you would most likely want to fully explore the physical elements of earth-plane existence, because the senses would be like a new toy. The warmth of a fire, the soothing feel of water, the magic of air, and the comfort of trees would draw you naturally with a sense of awe and delight.

Eventually you would start to understand the fatigue life can bring, and you might fail in living up to your ideals once in a while, because you would start to feel the pain of loss. As an angel now human, you would miss loved ones when they go away. Human life would teach you how humans fear that we are not good enough, how we are not doing enough, and how we kick and torment ourselves when opportunities pass. If you were an angel who took the risk to be a human, you would see what it is like to go after a dream and get lost along the way.

For an angel, figuring out money and the concept of worth would be particularly difficult, because it is so arbitrary, yet so important to being human. Angels have watched us chase after money, better jobs, better relationships, and better love. They have watched as we chose security and boredom over rich experiences. Many times they have tried to attract our attention and get us to stop and take note of a beautiful sunset that we just ignored. They have been frustrated when we forgot to look up and witness a beautiful cloud painting they have created just for us. Angels have noted the days when our childlike wonder was replaced by worries and stress.

Angels wonder why we would insult God by thinking there is some perfection to attain in our physical appearance, as if it were some sort of key to happiness. They know that imperfections are the openings for the Holy Spirit. Angels cannot understand why more people don't enjoy getting old and keeping childlike wonder alive. Angels probably cringe each time we let pride take precedence over love. We often take our problems so seriously that we cloud the solutions, rays of hope, and positive outcomes that the angels are trying to show us. In our obsession with time, we forget that this very moment is always one of the most glorious opportunities God has ever bestowed on us. From the perspective of the angels, there are so many simple things we could do to make life a heavenly experience.

So, we can come to a couple of conclusions: Maybe it is best for the angels to stay where they have their beautiful perspective of the gift of human life, where they hold the vision for us and help encourage us to find ways to enjoy our time while we are here, knowing that they are welcome to enjoy life with us. Our part of the deal requires that we get to a place where we can be present to the inspiration the angels send our way. When we establish a sacred place within us where we meet the angels, we can allow ourselves to see visions with new eyes, and to open our hearts to Divine Love, all the while honoring what it truly means to be a human. Many humans want to be like the angels, or imagine themselves to be angels. This is great. It's important, however, to remember that the angels spend all their time praising and loving God; that is all they do. If we were to do this in our lives — and it isn't as easy as you think — we would be living the way the angels do.

CHAPTER THREE

Cultivating Resonant Qualities

I will not wish thee riches nor the glow of greatness, but that wherever thou go some weary heart shall gladden at thy smile, or shadowed life know sunshine for a while. And so thy path shall be a track of light, like angels' footsteps passing through the night.

— WORDS ON A CHURCH WALL IN UPWALTHAM, ENGLAND

One essential and simple key to happiness is to focus outside ourselves and give to others. This doesn't mean to neglect ourselves and exhaust all our energy helping others. It means that we create a balance, so that our focus expands beyond needy human issues. Without our spiritual center, we can become like hungry ghosts, grasping to feed on any pleasurable energy we perceive, but never reaching gratification or fulfillment. Cultivating qualities that resonate with a high frequency brings true fulfillment, and creates an ever-present fresh energy flow that feeds our soul. The angels represent our higher nature, and they are the caretakers of divine qualities.

Buddhism teaches a set of precepts to live by. A *precept* is a rule, instruction, or principle that guides our actions and moral behavior. Practicing the precepts involves three dimensions: form, which means grasping the idea; practice, in that once we understand the form we then put it to use; and, equally important, spirit, which entails internalizing the inner spirit of the precept so that practicing it comes from an authentic place.

Similarly, living a life that reflects angel consciousness entails the cultivation of divine qualities. Divine qualities are simply what the angels respond to, and it is our part of the bargain to help the angels keep these qualities alive on the planet by embodying them fully. Remember, the angels are our cocreative partners in life. To allow their beneficial influence, we are called on to develop qualities that "angel nature" vibrates to. Which qualities would the angels, with their high vibrational frequency, naturally resonate to? Love, peace, gratitude, humor, joy, and compassion all come immediately to mind.

Think about it. If we are brimming with anger, resentment, and hatred, and these qualities have become too familiar and too comfortable to give up, where will the angels find room to dance in our consciousness? If we continually do things that repress our souls, how can the angels participate in our lives and inspire our creative spirits? The angels don't leave us, but our behavior can certainly make it difficult for them to interact with us. The angels wait in love for the moment when we choose to let go of the weights we have been dragging around and look to the Divine. Then they rejoice because on our own we have made the choice to change our hearts — it wasn't forced on us.

Basics

A quality (trait, attribute, feature, property, condition, distinctive character) can be cultivated. According to *The American Heritage Dictionary*, the word *cultivate* means "1. To improve and prepare (land) for raising crops. 2. To grow or tend (a plant or a crop). 3. To form and refine, as by education. 4. To seek the acquaintance or good will of." The word origin is the Latin *colere*, which means to inhabit, worship, develop, and be busy.

First and foremost, for anything to be cultivated and to grow, a seed has to be planted in fertile ground. Many qualities have a divine impulse to tune in to. Some of these qualities seem to be universal, and some are very personal. When you start living them, you will recognize the qualities that *feel* like a direct link to the angels. This is not a judgment call. In other words, these qualities relate to the Divine because the experience of them creates a higher vibration, a harmonic that the angels respond to. I did not decide that they were divine; they are simply words representing natural ways to have direct experiences of the Divine.

Natural goodness is intrinsic. It leads to good outcomes, and sends positive constructive vibrations far and wide. Creating natural goodness means creating positive, uplifting vibrations. This doesn't mean you go around blissfully out of touch with what is happening down here on earth; it means that you learn to navigate and stay on course by being in the moment and taking care of the moment — remembering to include your divinity in each decision. By integrating divine qualities into our human experience, we champion our own guardian angels, and in turn receive many blessings.

Our Actions Speak for Our Consciousness

One of the important things to remember is that the way we attract angels is by becoming the qualities that are of interest to them. When we focus on such qualities as compassion, faith, or tolerance, we attract angelic beings that are trying to help develop that in all humanity.

— K. MARTIN-KURI

We have to consciously give out divine qualities to receive them. If you ask God in prayer for an angelic quality, such as forgiveness, then it is crucial to pay attention to all the times, and all the ways, it is required directly from you. If you are practicing gratitude, you are called upon to take it to heart. If you want abundance, you cannot live with a mentality of hoarding. Cultivating divine qualities requires an innate willingness to allow the angels to guide you in all the ways you are called to practice these qualities — and in the way you personally carry the energy.

Angels are here to lead us to our higher selves and to God, and at the same time allow us to honor the experience of being human, without dismissing the physical realm. The angels are not asking us to become angels or pure spirit, but to become more angelic in our very humanity. Making a move toward being more angelic gives us a deeper wisdom we may not have thought we were capable of, and allows us to view our nobility from a divine perspective. Best of all, every once in a while, for no reason, we happen upon moments of happiness and bliss that are like nothing else in this world.

Grace Happens

> *Things of heaven cannot be attained by perseverance; they are the grace of God. To open to this and trust in it is how belief is crystallized into faith. We cannot pay for it in any form, in any way, by our goodness, by our piety, by our great qualities, merits, or virtues; nothing. It is a gift, and all we can do is receive it.*
>
> — HAZRAT INAYAT KHAN

In a state of grace, one feels in tune with and in good favor with Divine Providence. What better place to be than in a state of grace! But grace cannot be captured and possessed; it visits us with love and then moves on, leaving us feeling blessed. When the angels bless our consciousness, our hearts begin to open like flowers with infinite petals, and we discover a new depth to life and love.

We cannot demand that grace come to us, and it's the same with angels. We can know them, but we cannot demand that they do something for us. Yet there are things we can do that put us in a better position to be present for grace and for angels. Step one is to realize that a special consciousness exists connected with the state of grace. If we pay attention with our hearts, we will recognize it. If we take the time to have reverence for the world we live in, we will be blessed by it.

One of the most beautiful things about grace and the angels is that they are unearned. They do not come because we have followed a set of rules, they do not visit us because we have been good little girls and boys, and they can never be bought or controlled by us. Like anything beautiful, if we chase them we will end up with the experience of just missing them; it will feel as if we got there too late. We don't need to chase after God and the angels; they are right here, and so is amazing grace.

One afternoon my friend Jai and I were driving the back roads of Ojai — a special place in California — listening to a Judy Collins tape. Just as we approached our favorite pond, nestled at the foot of a beautiful mountain range, the song "Amazing Grace" began to play. I stopped the car and turned off the motor, but kept the music playing loudly. We quietly stepped out of the car and stood on a little hill by the pond. We watched in reverence as a flock of birds appeared, hundreds of them, and the birds began to fly over the pond in a ballet of beauty, moving to the music of "Amazing Grace." Time stood still. The sky, the clouds, the mountain range, and the ground we were standing on took on a heightened sense of beauty — the angels were with us. I experienced a deep understanding and acceptance of life in that timeless moment.

Everything was intrinsically okay; everything in the air seemed blessed by love. Life and death became the same. I felt that I was one of the birds flying, I was the water in the pond reflecting the surrounding beauty, I was the music sending its powerful vibrations out into the ether. I knew in that moment what death of the body is — a merging with the cosmic spirit of life. Nothing to fear, unless you are afraid of feeling pure love and peace.

I feel so grateful to have been blessed with many moments of this kind of grace. Grace happens anywhere and anytime the angels have a moment to directly merge with us. I have been in groups of people who have come together to honor the angels, and we've been lifted to unimaginable heights. I have been alone, doing nothing out of the ordinary, and felt their incredible love. It happens sometimes when I am out and about and I meet the eyes of a baby or small child. You cannot expect or seek these heightened moments, because grace is not like that. It just happens.

Being gracious is another aspect of grace. To be gracious means to be naturally kind and compassionate, refined and pleasant. The angels serve as good examples of graciousness. They are gracious by nature and can help us come to a point of inner peace so that our graciousness is honest and real. When you act graciously, do it for the angels, not to win favor from other humans. Never think of what you are not getting from others, but rather know that the angels are always ready to give you a moment of graceful bliss.

My late, great friend Kip had a deep, shamanlike connection with the angels and devas of nature. To counteract a popular bumper sticker, he had bumper stickers printed that read: "Grace Happens." Always remember, grace happens.

Gratitude

You can clean your aura and raise your vibration by giving thanks. The resonance of gratitude in your body vibrates with your heart center. It allows you to open to receive more.

— SANAYA ROMAN

Being a living, breathing human is truly a miracle and gift. Sometimes, though, life becomes full of stress and strain, and we tend to just push through and neglect the here and now, especially if we perceive it to be full of painful observations. The here and now is where our souls are known and accepted. It is where our spirits soar freely. The true way to live in continuous flow with the angels is to adopt the "gratitude attitude." When we are grateful to be alive, the world no longer seems like a place of doom; it becomes a beautiful, unfolding landscape of heaven. So when the now becomes too much, we can give it up to gratitude, and the chemistry of the now will change and we will feel safe. Whereas grace is a gift from God and the angels, gratitude is our response. Gratitude is also the queen of divine qualities, because it is so easy for us to practice, and the results are so quick.

The word *grateful* comes from the Latin word *gratus*, which means pleasing and thankful. From this Latin word we also get *congratulate, grace, gratuity, gratify,* and *gratis*. What does being grateful really mean? We know that it means appreciating something; it means that we are pleased by an event, or that we have received something freely — gratis. The word *appreciate* means to estimate the quality or value of something, to value highly and to increase in value or price, to cherish, prize, and treasure. How much do you appreciate yourself and this gift of life? Do you ever have moments of overwhelming gratitude for the priceless, free grace of God's love?

Take a moment to stop reading and begin to be thankful for all the wonderful things around you. Make this into a prayer, and as you thank the Great Creator, consciously love what you are grateful for. If you have been unaccustomed to noticing all that is good in your life, you may need to start out slowly; don't worry if it seems difficult at first.

Sometimes when I want to change the chemistry of my mind-set to get into the space to write, I begin by thanking God for everything I see around me. I thank God for the clothes I am wearing, for the books scattered around me, for the beauty of the color rays I am surrounded with, for the sustenance that gives me energy, and for the body that allows me to interact physically with life. Then I begin to thank God for all the frustrations and obstacles I perceive, the troubles and the attachments; I do this because I know that these great teachers will eventually bring me a lighter view of life.

The alchemy of gratitude happens when we begin to appreciate the gift of life as opposed to feeling entitled to life. When we embrace the full experience of being a human on God's green earth, gratitude is our natural and prayerful response. The Tibetan Buddhists believe that a human life is a hard-won chance to evolve and learn the right way to live. If a human lifetime is thoughtlessly wasted in mere survival activities, the chance to move toward enlightenment in the future will be further out of reach. The Buddha said, "Once the human lifetime has been lost, it will be as hard to find another as it is for an old blind turtle in the great ocean who surfaces every hundred years to come up by chance with his neck through a single golden yoke that floats randomly around in the vast ocean."

Gratitude creates a "great attitude." Creating gratitude can be an ongoing meditation you can practice all day long. I try to remember to thank everything I encounter. When I am writing on my computer and I get the program to perform a special function, I thank it when I finish. I thank my car for getting me places. I thank the musicians for the music I listen to. I mentally thank flowers for reminding me of the angels. I thank my cats for being so funny. I thank the water I use to drink and bathe in. I thank the sun for its warmth. I thank the angels. I find that when I engage in this process of thanking, I feel happier and lighter throughout the day. I am able to pause and be grateful for the amazing process of life, and this helps me appreciate and be conscious of the angels.

The words *Thank you, God* can become a powerful prayer when they come from the heart. These words can be a mantra you use all day long; this mantra will attract the miraculous like nothing else, simply because you will be in the position — the mind-set — to recognize the miraculous. If you have trouble with gratitude, don't be hard on yourself, and don't forget to ask for help from the angels. Gratitude is attuned to a highly refined vibrational level of the angels. When you seek this vibration, your seeking alerts the angels, and they begin helping you change your heart.

Gratitude can also change worry alchemically. When you are worried over something, hand it over to God with thanksgiving.

Do not fret or have any anxiety about anything, but in every circumstance and in everything, by prayer and petition (definite requests), with thanksgiving, continue to make your wants known to God.

— PHILIPPIANS 4:6

Years ago my friend Shannon used to put on classical music and sing "Thank you, God" to the music. She got me doing this too, and every now and then when I hear beautiful music these words come strongly into my mind and fill my heart with joy.

PRACTICE IDEAS

1. Make a little gratitude box, or journal, and write what you are thankful for each day. Acknowledge things you are not particularly grateful for, and thank God for them too, with the intention of changing your feelings about them. Then periodically read about your gratitude transformations.

2. Celebrate thanksgiving once a month. Call up all your loved ones and thank them for being in your life, or send out thank-you notes with a similar message.

3. Meditate on gratitude. Visualize yourself and your beauty and thank God that your inner light is charged with love. Let God know you are

willing to live a miraculous life. Know that
miracles happen whenever love touches you with
its divine vibration. Remember that at the heart
of any matter is the simple fact that love is the
healer.

Love

Love vibrates rapidly. Fear has a slower rate of vibration.
Those who channel fearful energies find that as time passes,
the fear vibration grows heavy, depressing. Eventually, it
brings sleep, gloominess, discouragement, despair. The love
vibration brings enthusiasm, energy, interest, perception.
This is what will heal the world: clear and undistorted
perception, flowing through a you that is not self-reflective
in the egoic sense, but self-reflective in the sense of knowing
the God within.

— KEN CAREY, *RETURN OF THE BIRD TRIBES*

Love is an energy that flows through us from the Creator outward. We cannot withhold love or try to manipulate or control with it. Love is pure divine energy, and if we are willing
to allow it to flow through us, it will travel far and wide, with
our own divine essence included. Trouble comes when we
block a channel for love to come through freely and joyously.
Maybe we perceive a good reason for blocking this channel —
a reason why we are not able to love — but this is not so.
There are no good reasons for blocking love, and if we allow
ourselves to be a channel for Divine Love, we are able to love

all. Love is always waiting at the doorway of our hearts for an opening to flow through. If we resist, we may feel as if a great pressure is on us. It is difficult to stop the course of a river, and it is difficult to stop the course of love. Don't muddy the waters of love by trudging heavily through life, worrying and blocking love with imagined foes.

A guiding principle that keeps me on course is to realize that when our time to leave this physical experience comes, we will be asked, "How well did you love?" I doubt any of our business deals will be mentioned; the type of car we drove will not be of any importance. What will be celebrated throughout eternity are all the loving moments we shared.

WAVES OF LOVE MEDITATION

Prepare a quiet moment and experience a soften-the-blocks love meditation. Sit quietly, and begin to tune into the divine energy of love. Imagine waves of love flowing to earth from the Creator. Imagine a circular pattern, flowing to earth, then to heaven, and back again. Stand under a wave of love and feel it begin to flow through an opening in your soul. Feel the angels crowd around you, protecting you with their colorful love. Is the opening in your heart? Your crown? Your back? Sense where the opening is — it's up to you. Just allow an opening.

Is the love flowing out through your hands, heart, head, and eyes? Do you feel the energy getting stuck anywhere? If so, allow information to come to you that will bring you understanding. Release the block, and let love with its powerful energy melt the block and transmute its underlying causes.

Think of those you love, and soften any blocks you feel toward them. Love can reach across any number of miles. It can even touch those who have passed over to other realms. Allow love to reach into your soul and create smiles, tears, tingles, joy, and blessings. Continue this as long as you like, and keep at it until you feel that your channels for love are clearing. Remember, there is no such thing as conditional love. Conditions — blocks — have nothing to do with love. Love is the highest and most available energy in the universe.

Humility

Human survival depends on whether we are brave enough to face the full desolation of what we have done to our psyches and the planet, and wise and humble enough to turn to the Divine inside and outside us to learn what we will need to go forward.

— ANDREW HARVEY

Being human is a complex experience, to say the least. Awakening our spiritual nature gives us a view of being human that goes beyond our physical space and our selfish desires. If we don't redefine ourselves once we begin awakening, big conflicts arise in our lives. One of the biggest has to do with pride. Pride is a mixed bag, in that we need to *feel* proud once in a while, but *being* proud can mean being stubbornly attached to a narrow point of view. So we can change the chemistry of the feeling of pride to consciously loving the Divine within us. Instead of feeling proud that we did something great, we acknowledge the Divine Creator and give thanks that we are gifted with the ability to transform the world with our love. In other words, we constantly acknowledge that our time here on earth is by the grace of God; it is sacred time. We always stand on holy ground; our body is a temple in which the light of God dwells.

Etymologically speaking, *humble* means close to the ground, coming from *humus*, which is the Latin word for earth. There is no way to ignore how humble — how close to the ground —we really are. Human life is an earthly experience. The humus, the soil of the earth, is what sustains us. Our bodies are made from the same elements as the ground on which we build houses, pave roads, destroy forests, and fashion comfort for our survival. We can spend most of our time here trying to escape in one way or another, but the fact is that the human race has very little chance of survival if there is not a massive spiritual transformation of values — a letting go of the excessive pride of thinking that humans are all-powerful. Mother Nature humbles us often. Earthquakes, storms, and a basic understanding of her natural laws make us realize how powerless we are in the face of our changing planet.

I believe our first real glimpse of being awake and conscious comes through humility. Humility, like gratitude, is a powerful alchemical essence. When we truly humble ourselves and get down on our knees on the sacred humus, then we are raised up in spirit to unimaginable heights. Sometimes we have to go down before we can go up. Sometimes we have to go within before we can operate consciously outside. Opening to humility is an ongoing process, facilitated through prayerful communication with God and playing with the angels. Praying with humility and gratitude offers a direct line to God. Prepare your inner soil; give the humus of your soul the humble richness it needs to present you with the real treasures of heaven.

Cultivating the Antidote to Seriousness

*Not a shred of evidence exists in favor of the idea
that life is serious.*

— BRENDAN GILL

Sometimes the best way to release a problem is to realize that
in the big picture our problems are really very small. We can
always change the chemistry of our problems by bringing the
angels around for a good laugh. The angels want us to "get a
life" and "get over it." This does not mean that we carelessly
disregard the painful issues in our lives, but simply that we
don't let the heaviness rule our overall response to life. There
is always time to take care of our pain and our issues, but it is
important to understand that pain and issues are not what
defines us. Our pain is not who we are. We are interesting,
complex beings who have a multidimensional response to life.
Throughout the course of a day, we may experience several
different emotional responses; sometimes we feel angry but
happy at the same time. Sometimes sadness comes when we are
basically joyful. The point is we don't need to define ourselves
by moods or emotions. Moods and emotions want to move on;
they do not want to take up residence in our minds. Let the
changing landscape of your heart and mind move like the passing clouds that create beautiful angel art in the sky above.

People can waste a great deal of time taking life seriously
and worrying about perceived problems. My friend Charlie
reached a period in his life when he felt burdened by his problems. He spent most of his time worrying with great seriousness about what he was going to do. While driving on some

treacherous mountain curves one day, pondering the serious issues he faced, he took one curve too fast and found himself looking down several hundred feet of mountain with his van up on two wheels. In that instant, Charlie realized that he was probably going to die and that all the issues he was worried about would never be resolved. Then a sudden force — his guardian angel, no doubt — pulled Charlie's van back into control, and he was saved from imminent death. After the shock subsided, he found himself laughing hysterically at how absurd all his worry was. Nothing seemed so serious anymore; suddenly, he was struck by how funny everything was, and he laughed and laughed. Charlie realized that the moments he had spent worrying were wasted time, which could just as easily have been spent in enjoyment.

Those of us who become consumed with the illusion of seriousness in our lives usually reach a turning point. Sometimes this turning point happens dramatically, as in a near-death experience; other times, it happens less dramatically, as in a sudden realization that you have spent weeks and months without having any fun. If you are not planning to have a near-death experience any time soon but you are plagued by seriousness, pay attention to the time and energy you spend on seriousness. Start by writing down all the serious issues you are dealing with in your life at the moment. Now look at how funny these issues look on paper, and let yourself laugh out loud. If the issues don't strike you as funny and you can't bring yourself to laugh, just look for some aspect of humor and lightness, however small. When we start laughing at our lives, sometimes we end up hysterical, and we may cry, scream, or shout out the window. The point is we need a release now and then, and laughter is a good one.

Give up, give in, and let go. Pretend that you are filled

with helium and that the only things keeping you on the ground are the serious issues in your life; let yourself rise above them for a different perspective. If you've seen the movie *Mary Poppins*, think back to the scene with the song "I Love to Laugh"; the more people laughed, the higher they rose, until they reached the ceiling. When they wanted to come down, they had to think of something sad and heavy. Take a break from the seriousness of life; the angels will encourage it. Remember that old Scottish saying: "Angels can fly because they take themselves lightly."

Laughter has many benefits. It exercises the lungs, it releases superfluous energy, it bathes your body in endorphins (natural pain relievers), and it promotes healing. You might want to take a look at *Anatomy of an Illness* by the renowned writer Norman Cousins, who cured himself of a serious illness through laughter and humor. If you need help bringing laughter into your life, start by surrounding yourself with humor. Do your own study on humor. Make a list of the movies, comedians, television shows, books, friends, and situations that make you laugh, and always search for more.

In your angel journal, keep track of the humor and seriousness in your life. If you catch yourself becoming plagued by seriousness, examine your behavior and that of others. Find out what keeps happening in your life that isn't funny. Whenever you like, ask the angels to release you from seriousness and connect you with humor. The plague of seriousness is everywhere: in our churches and schools, on the news, and at work. It is hard to escape from it. But there is always a way to introduce humor into any situation, and you may need to be the instigator.

Angels are antiserious; there is no weight in their realm, and they simply can't take anything seriously. This means that they can't take us or our problems seriously. This doesn't mean they ignore our problems; they will do what they can to help us remove the serious worries so that we can solve problems creatively and take ourselves lightly. *The Oxford American Dictionary* defines *serious* as solemn and thoughtful, not smiling, not casual or lighthearted, causing great concern, and of grave and somber disposition. How could anyone want to be serious after reading that?

PRACTICE IDEAS

1. List all the serious issues you face at the moment, and laugh at them.

2. Take a laughter inventory, and find new ways to laugh. Also, learn how to have a good hearty laugh as often as possible.

3. Keep a trash bag page in your angel journal for serious trash that you want removed from your life, such as worries, negative thoughts, and negative personalities. Then take out the trash.

Happiness Training

Happiness is not in our circumstances but in ourselves. It is not something we see, like a rainbow, or feel, like the heat of a fire. Happiness is something we are.

— JOHN SHEERIN

How many times have you heard yourself or someone else say, "When such and such happens, I'll be happy"? Well, it doesn't

work that way; first you have to learn how to be happy now —
without reason. Happiness without reason is the ultimate freedom. This freedom from conditions and contingencies means
that you aren't waiting for the right ingredients to make you
happy; you just *are* happy. No matter what the circumstances,
you feel blessed and happy. If you are truly happy without reason, you are freed from the domination of outward conditions.
You are free to live happily in the present tense, in the now.

Happiness without reason requires training. The state of
happiness requires that you know yourself and that you identify precise moments when you switch from being happy and
at ease on this planet to being uncomfortable and out of synch.

The problem with true happiness is that there is no key to
its door; there are no rules to follow, no steps to take, and no
conditions for it to exist. There is no manual or cookbook
with recipes to read. True happiness is a state of grace. It's a
bit like having a naturally occurring chemical in your blood-
stream that feeds your brain and bathes your soul in positive
energy. There is nothing to swallow, breathe, look at, smell,
or do to become happy. Happiness comes and goes. We cannot plan it; it is a naturally occurring product of living in the
present tense, free from external conditions. We can, however, train ourselves to be *available* and *open* to happiness.

Happiness training involves accepting everything the
angels have to teach: humor, love, beauty, lightness of being,
and joy. It requires living in the now and being *awake*. You
need to get off autopilot. Autopilot is a personality program
some of us adopt to elude pain and to avoid living and experiencing the now. By subscribing to set routines and predictable
patterns, some people are sleepwalking through the day. You
won't find these people rocking the boat or moving and shaking

the world; in their minds, that isn't safe. Going on autopilot does not get rid of the pain and suffering in your life; it only delays and diffuses it. Sooner or later, the voids will come back to haunt the person on automatic pilot. When we see children on autopilot, we call it mental illness. Young children normally don't resist life. When they feel like crying, laughing, screaming, or singing, they just do it. As I've said, angels and children go together; they are happy and creative. Angels see this happy state as the way we are meant to be — all of us.

TRAINING STEPS TO HAPPINESS

1. Step number one of happiness training is: Get off autopilot. Wake up and experience your senses. Stop and smell the roses; wake up and smell the coffee. Stop any automatic behavior that keeps you from experiencing life. Autopilot behavior is a way of resisting life and avoiding pain; it avoids the present.

   Happiness (or unhappiness) is largely a result and function of how we *relate* and *react* to events in our lives; it does not reside in the circumstances or the events themselves. Overreacting to an adverse event makes it worse. Overinterpreting circumstances with an attitude of what "should be" according to a given set of conditions is a sure way to deter happiness. It's crucial that we learn not to react with fear, anger, or disappointment to the events of the day. We can choose to see whatever arises in the moment with fascination and interest, and know that it is neither good nor bad. Events and things are only bad or wrong when they are compared to a standard in your imagination of what should be.

2. Step number two of happiness training is: Adopt a sense of lightness and humor in every situation you encounter, and the angels will be there to help. Do not overreact to or overinterpret situations that come your way.

    The happy mind is free of judgments, expectations, and worries concerning other people. Other people's actions can only hurt us when we have a preconceived notion of their intent toward us. When we are happy with ourselves, then we can see others as innocent. If someone sends you a carton of horse manure, just assume they forgot the horse! Worrying about people doesn't help them or you. Expecting people to behave in certain ways will only disappoint you. Judging yourself and others is a waste of time.

3. Step number three of happiness training is: Don't let other people affect your happiness. Just as events are neither good nor bad, the same is true of people; see people and their actions as interesting and fascinating, originating from a source of innocence. Get past taking anything personally. In most situations, people and circumstances can only hurt you if you let them.

    Go and love some more. Giving love on any level is a sure way to happiness. This love must be unconditional love, of course, and, as always, with giving you receive. Anne Frank once said, "Whoever is happy will make others happy too. He who has courage and faith will never perish in misery!" Have the courage and faith to spread your happiness and love around, and you will create an abundance that continues to give throughout the universe. Love and happiness are synergistic; their combined effects exceed the sum of their individual effects.

4. Step number four of happiness training is: Be generous with your love and happiness; spread it throughout the universe. Love, and do as you will. Give from your abundance of happiness. As David Grayson says, "Make one person happy each day and in forty years you have made 14,600 human begins happy for a little time at least."

Unconditional happiness is the ultimate freedom. It doesn't require that you live anywhere special, that you dress a certain way, that you ingest a mind-altering substance, or that you do anything other than make yourself available to receive it, anytime and anyplace. Happiness has been described as a butterfly; when you pursue it, it is always just beyond reach, but if you sit quietly it may alight upon you. Angels are natural happiness trainers, so sit down quietly and ask them to help you develop a habit of happiness.

Harmony

Only those who partake of the harmony within their souls know the harmony that runs through nature.

— PARAMAHANSA YOGANANDA

If you know even a little bit about music and its structure and why we enjoy it, you know about harmony. When musical notes don't harmonize, this creates a tense, harsh, or discordant sound. Such a sound can be interesting and create excitement, so I am not saying here that harmony is good and discordance necessarily bad; creativity can embrace both.

Each of us has an inner note that our soul sings. When we are in tune with the Divine, our note resonates with the harmony of heaven and the choirs of angels. We can use this idea in our personal relationships. We find ourselves in harmony with some people, and others seem to be part of a different scale.

Harmonious living means forming a pleasing or consistent whole, free from disagreement or ill feeling. To create a harmonious whole with our lives and the people we encounter, we need to find the point of harmony between us and them. Of course, we can learn much from those who don't harmonize with our inner note, but the more aware we are of what is going on, the better we can create harmony in our lives, which may mean keeping a healthy distance from certain people. We will notice harmony best if we allow ourselves to open our hearts more. If we find that there is no harmony and that all we see is drama or dysfunction, we can choose to keep this discordance out of our inner sanctums.

When we practice a spiritual life and include prayer, contemplation, meditation, spiritual study, self-awareness, compassion, and service as constant parts of our lives, we are resonating to a spiritual scale of musical notes. When we encounter people who are not practicing spiritual lives, even if they say they are, our notes won't resonate harmonically. If we try to work in partnership with someone who is only in it for money and glamour, and we are in it for love, service, and creativity, we won't find harmony.

Have you ever noticed how colors don't clash in nature? We can mix purples, oranges, yellows, and reds along with greens, and as long as the combination is part of nature it will never clash. Well, if we are natural and spiritual, it won't matter how many different notes we bring together; as long as we are in tune with the Divine, we will be in harmony. All of this is another idea to play with for understanding.

GET A TUNE-UP

Keep your inner note strong by keeping it in tune. You can do this by staying true to yourself and not trying to fit with another note that is not in harmony with yours. Ask the angels to remind you when you need to tune up your inner note.

Listen to the chord struck between two souls. Think of relationships you have in your life, and go into a meditative state with the angels. Get in touch with your own inner note. It is okay if you don't hear a tone — just use your imagination. Now listen to the notes of other people in your life. Do they harmonize? After you meditate on harmony, write about your thoughts. If you find that you don't harmonize with someone, think about why. The answer is probably a matter of values clashing.

If you put your heart into them, your creativity and your life will resonate with other hearts and attract true appreciation.

Investigate harmonic resonance in your own life and in your creative expression. You may find that leading a harmonious life will get you in touch with the key that unlocks the door to your creative heart center. The angels know right where this key is at all times.

Create your own "harmonic convergence" in your life with the angels.

Patience into Peace

Let nothing disturb you; nothing frighten you.
All things are passing.
God never changes.
Patience obtains all things.
Nothing is wanting to him who possesses God.
God alone suffices.

— St. Teresa's Bookmark

Saint Teresa said, "Patience obtains all things." What she meant is that in time you will have everything you need, and you will learn to want what you have. The magic behind patience is that it means we have backed off from a situation — we have decided "to let go and let God." We are letting time do us a favor. To cultivate patience as a divine experience, we need to be comfortable with giving up our need for control, and we need to find the faith that there is a divine force of wisdom that can sort things out for us in beautiful ways we had not thought of.

Being patient is a form of inner battle, because if you have to define yourself as patient, then there is something stirring in you to be impulsive, to express something, or to act out. To *be* a patient means to be someone who is suffering. The definition of *patient* as an adjective means to bear affliction with calmness, and it comes from the Latin *pati*, suffer, which is also the origin of the words *passion* and *passive*.

You've heard the saying "Patience is a virtue." The word *virtue* means moral excellence, righteousness, and conformity to standard morality or mores. The origin of *virtue* comes from the Latin *virtus* — bravery, strength, skill — which came from the Latin *vir*, which means man. We have been beaten up a bit with the notion of virtue. We have high standards we feel we must live up to, set by people who are ready to control the behavior of society so they will be safe, but who seem unwilling to do anything about the roots of the behavior. Of course virtue is something to strive for, but in a natural way, and not by way of conforming to some loud humans' set of standards. Virtue needs to be measured in a divine way, by God knowing what is in our hearts and by us feeling good about what is filling our hearts. So let's look beyond patience as a virtue; that is a trap, which too often means we don't want to hear what is trying to speak from within. As I said before, we would not need patience if there wasn't something needing expression from a place within us.

When we are feeling impatient, it's wise to meet our impatience face-to-face, so that it won't build up into something else. Often we try to be patient, and we fail — because we are "trying," not doing. We are not paying attention to the inner messages the angels are sending us. What does our impatience want to tell us? When we find out, do we need to act on it? If so, what would be the best way? Wisdom is our only tool in this regard. To get to the wisdom of a situation, it's important to take time out to meditate on the situation. Ask the angels to help position you for the best and highest outcome. Angels want us to merge into divine qualities on our own. They can hold the vision for us, but they can't make the changes for us. We are the ones who decide to change and go to new heights. As soon as we make this simple choice, they will guide us as best they can.

BECOME THE ANGELS' PATIENT

After great loss, there is suffering; that is a fact of life. Another fact of life is that time really does heal — it makes whole again. If you make the decision not to fight these facts and you realize that the angels are willing to help, then you will find peace. Peace *will* come to you, and there is really nothing better than a sense of mental peace, physical peace, spiritual peace, and inner peace.

To stay patient and calm, I highly recommend prayer. If you are suffering, if you feel your thoughts won't let you alone, begin to pray each time they start to run over you. Pretend you are a patient in the angels' hospital of love, and let them minister to you. Stay in your center of love, and each time you feel it leaving, stop and pray. Patience means you are praying. Be spontaneous with your prayers. Be like a child, and don't worry about the words in your prayers. God and the angels listen to your heart, and they answer prayers in time — though we may not realize exactly what we asked for.

Kindness

To love for the sake of being loved is human,
but to love for the sake of loving is Angelic.

— ALPHONSE DE LAMARTINE

When my niece, Jessica, was four years old, I asked her to tell me what she knew about angels. She told me some funny things, such as, "They probably glow in the dark...and, of course, we know they have feet." But most important, she told me she knew that angels love little kids. I agreed, and I asked her, since she was a little kid, if the angels had any messages for all of us here on earth. She quickly replied, "Yes. Be kind to others, and love one another!"

Soon after my discussion about angels with my niece (circa 1988), I had the chance to hear the Dalai Lama speak. If you don't know by now, the Dalai Lama is the spiritual leader of the Tibetan Buddhists, living in exile from his homeland. The overall feeling emanating from the entire audience lifted my soul from the minute I walked into the building. I had the privilege of sitting near the front of the auditorium, where the Tibetan families were sitting. The look on their faces when the Dalai Lama came out to speak was incredibly moving, and I felt like I had merged into their world. I felt a sense of true compassion, an ocean of love.

Basically, the Dalai Lama had the same message for us humans that my niece relayed from the angels. The title of his talk was "A Human Approach to World Peace." He talked about practicing compassion for others as a way to develop inner stability and a sense of responsibility for the human family. Compassion provides security and inner stamina and allows us to reduce fear and develop self-confidence with awareness. What the Dalai Lama means by compassion is actually altruism. When you show kindness and act upon a feeling of empathy toward a very poor person, your compassion is based on altruistic considerations. On the other hand, love toward your partner, lover, spouse, friend, or children is usually based on attachment. When the attachment changes, your kindness also changes, and may even disappear. Real love is based not on attachment, but on altruism.

The Dalai Lama said that the main source of supreme happiness and joy is mental stability and mental peace. Several things can interfere with mental peace. One such thing is anger. The Dalai Lama said that anger diminishes mind —

that is, it is of no use at all and appears as protection from something that *might* happen. Anger deceives us. A person can destroy your property, your body, your friends, and all the supposed sources of your happiness, but real mental stability and peace of mind cannot be destroyed, unless your brain is physically injured. We are minds; we are consciousness. The real enemies to our peace of mind are not external people or events, but internal states, such as anger.

The foundation for solving human problems lies in transforming human attitudes. If we are happy, truly happy without external reasons, with our minds at peace, then we can give kindness and love to other people effortlessly because we are drawing upon an unlimited energy source.

Since my first encounter with the Dalai Lama in 1988, I have attended several amazing events he has been involved in, and I've developed an addiction to hearing him laugh. In 1999 I had the privilege of shaking hands with him.

Random Angel Testing

Do not forget or neglect or refuse to extend hospitality to strangers [in the brotherhood — being friendly, cordial, and gracious, sharing the comforts of your home and doing your part generously], for through it some have entertained angels without knowing it.

— HEBREWS 13:2

When we consciously set out to cultivate divine qualities, the angels occasionally provide pop quizzes to let us know how we are doing. It may seem dangerous these days to acknowledge strangers in any way, especially to be hospitable to them, but most of us have developed a way of knowing intuitively when we are in danger. If you know and believe that you are protected, being friendly and helpful to strangers in the proper circumstances can be fun and quite enlightening. I'm not suggesting that you do anything unintelligent, such as thawing out a frozen snake in an act of kindness and then getting bitten. Within the grounds of safety, however, being kind will bring you great rewards. Responding kindly will also serve as an ongoing test, so to speak, with the angels themselves as the proctors.

One day, I was sitting in my car at a stoplight when I saw a strange-looking guy on a bike in my rearview mirror. My first reaction was to ignore him. He looked like he was in his fifties, and he was dressed up like a movie cowboy. He rode right up to the stoplight, which seemed to be taking a very long time to change to green, and he was now parallel with my open window on the passenger side of the car. So, I turned and smiled at him, and in return he smiled a beatific smile and said, "Greetings from the Master."

I was so astonished at what I heard that of course I had to ask, "What?"

So he repeated it: "Greetings from the Master."

I said thank you and continued smiling. The light changed, and I looked around to find that he had disappeared. I felt a tremendous rush of happy and joyful feelings. Later I realized that if I hadn't acknowledged this stranger, I would have missed out on a marvelous experience.

Sometimes, being aware of the ways of angels seems like belonging to a secret society where you never know when, where, and how another member of the organization will show up. If you feel like being rude or unkind to a stranger, be careful; he or she just might be an angel. Angels like to appear randomly at various locations to test our reactions. They usually do this in places you wouldn't normally identify with angels, such as gas stations, bars, airports, movie theaters, and street corners. The test itself is not serious. If we miss it or fail it, we have nothing to worry about. The only reason angels do random testing is to teach us love and respect for all human beings. They also want to wake us up to happiness and the joy of being alive.

Angels may give you hints or signs of an impending test. Things to watch for include an intense feeling of lightness in their presence; some form of radiance shining out from behind their eyes and a big smile; a knowing look — as if they know you and you know them from somewhere; a feeling of timelessness, as if you were suddenly in a movie or a different reality; a very distinctive, mirthful laugh, almost like tinkling bells and extremely contagious; a feeling that all the worldly events around you are ridiculous; and a stirring, sweet aroma resembling jasmine left behind after they disappear.

Continuing Education

I've elaborated on some of the divine qualities that cultivate a rich soil for the seeds we want to germinate for spiritual growth with the angels. There are many more divine qualities to explore with your angels. One great tool for this is to get a set of ANGEL® Cards (see the Resources section at the back of this book) and pick one randomly each day, then focus on it throughout the day. In your journal you can write a little statement on what the quality means to you. For example:

BEAUTY: I can only be inspired to write when I know I am immersed in beauty. Beauty is a healing force. Beauty is the energy dancing in my spirit.

The following is a sample list of qualities to play with.

Abundance	Humor
Balance	Integrity
Beauty	Joining the Dance of Life
Charity	Joy
Comfort	Light
Compassion	Love
Courage	Magnanimity
Divine Harmony	Might
Divinity	Original Innocence
Enthusiasm	Passion
Faith	Patience
Flexibility	Peace
Forgiveness	Play
Freedom	Redemption
Generosity	Reflection
Gentleness	Release
Goodness	Responsibility
Grace	Reverence
Gracefulness	Simplicity
Gratitude	Spontaneity
Happiness	Strength
Harmony	Truth
Healing	Understanding
Hope	Wisdom
Humility	Wonder

By cultivating and practicing these qualities, you naturally draw to you the angels who resonate with them. Enjoy!

CHAPTER FOUR

Nurturing Angel Practices

*Many great teachers, religious or otherwise, have walked
the earth, and from each one we can learn. Yet the angels,
from their vantage point and from their interplay with our
consciousness, can see what we truly are, can see the steps in
front of us, and continue to help us connect to our divine origin and goal. Now we can consciously seek their cooperation.*

— DOROTHY MACLEAN

*N*ow that you have created the mind-set and grasped the
vibrational levels of angel consciousness, and developed some of the divine qualities that resonate with angels, it
is time to establish practical ways to interact with the angels on
an ongoing basis. By encouraging you to develop practices that
resonate with the angels, I don't mean creating forced, regi-
mented, strict, or disciplined time when you stress yourself
trying to learn something or drill yourself until you can't take
it anymore. I mean having ongoing fun with the angels and
making your practices an exploration of joy and fun. By practicing with a sense of fun and exploration, you create a special
time where each practice is more than going over the "same old
stuff"; instead, it is a time to be open to the miraculous ways
of the angels.

With practice, you can become more "at one" with the
angels. If you are not enjoying yourself when you do a practice, stop and figure out why. We have enough stress and
"shoulds" in our lives, and we don't want to carry these into
our practice time with the angels. Now, we can't always
instantly turn off stress and guilt, but by engaging in practices
with the angels we can get past stress and instead nurture our
spiritual growth. I read an article recently that talked about
how we humans (especially women) are hardwired to nurture.

So the theory that tells us that after a stressful day at work we need time alone, or to plop down in front of the TV and vegetate, is actually physiologically incorrect. If we choose instead to come home and look forward to nurturing in some way — whether our loved ones, our pets, our gardens, or our creativity — the hormone oxytocin will be released. Oxytocin is a hormone that not only helps us to be peaceful but also helps us to create a bond, which in turn makes life meaningful.

For all of this to take root, we have to get away from the notion of a ticking clock pressuring us to accomplish who knows what. Instead, forget about the hours going by; if you take only one hour of your day to focus on your spiritual growth, and on nurturing what really matters to you, amazing things will happen. (That hour can be in the form of ten or twenty minutes here and there.) Eventually you will find your spiritual growth doesn't stop when you go out in the world; it expands. The angels are ever present.

The Guide Dance

Angels are heavenly guides. The word *guide* originates from the Germanic word *wit*, which means to know, and is related to the English equivalents *wise*, *wit*, and *witness*. It progressed from knowing to showing in the Germanic word *weisen*, to direct, show, indicate. The English word *guide* then evolved from the French equivalent of the Germanic *guider*. The dictionary definition of *guide* is to lead somebody in the right direction, and to advise or counsel somebody or influence the way somebody behaves.

Three words stand out from tracing the word origin of *guide*; these three words sum up how I feel the angels help guide us: *wise*, *wit*, and *witness*.

To be wise means to be able to make sensible decisions and judgments based on knowledge and experience — based on wisdom. The angels hold much wisdom concerning humans, because they have a unique view and perspective of us. And they have been around a long time.

Another thing to keep in mind is that there is a divine sense of humor in the universe, and that the angels are always ready to offer humorous associations in our daily lives when we allow their guidance to lighten our ways. This is their form of wit, always leavened by a healthy dose of good humor. The ability to laugh at ourselves is a wonderful gift we are born with.

> *The devil may act like a trickster, show wit, play the clown, dance a jig, and be a jokester, but the humus and humility of humor — never!*
>
> *The laughing recognition of one's own absurdity in the human comedy bans the devil as effectively as garlic and the cross.*
>
> — JAMES HILLMAN

The third word association for *guide* is *witness*. The angels witness what we choose to do in life; they witness how we feel, and they witness those times we risked a broken heart to love. They also witness our intentions and how we direct our energy.

> *We devas would like to dance around in the consciousness of every human being to wake you up to what you are.*
>
> — MESSAGE FROM THE TREE DEVAS
> RECEIVED BY DOROTHY MACLEAN

When you add *dance* to *guide*, you get *guidance* — something humans can't do without. If you see yourself dancing with life, you will know that sometimes you are dancing by yourself, with only the angels joining you. At other times, you are dancing in a group, and your movements depend on the group mind. Other times, you may engage in an intimate dance with a special partner. The cosmic dance of life can be slow, fast, lively, solemn, silent, loud, giving, taking — it is spiritual movement of the soul, spirit, and body. It is also more than just a physical movement or rhythm; it is a metaphor for spiritual living and relationships.

Dance to the beat of your own special music. Think of the world's various cultures; each has at least one special dance. Think of the freedom that dancing brings your soul. Dancing can be a way of praising the Creator. Appreciate dancing whenever you see it. Remember that the angels are dancing around in your consciousness, waking your soul up to the creative life force all around you. Join the cosmic dance of the universe. Watch your own dance of life and ask yourself if you need some added bounce in your step.

Dance is a form of play. Play is the golden key to truly learning anything and to expanding our creativity. What if we all had been allowed to learn everything with a sense of play? Think about it. Weren't we really just told what to learn and believe in school? Let's say every day the teacher brought in art materials, books, and creative props that somehow represented something we were studying and said, "Okay, class, let's spend the day playing with these so we can learn about such and such." What do you think would happen? My fantasy is that all the students would become teachers through their own creativity, and the class would teach itself with the main teacher directing. I also believe that teaching by play would allow people the freedom and courage to search for their own unique answers. This type of teaching is being practiced in a few innovative classrooms today. The main point is that we learn through play. This is why some children develop basic computer skills so quickly: They see computers as toys and feel free to play with them.

You were a child once and you had a natural tendency to play at all times. That child that you were is still part of you now. And that child is trying to get the message through to the adult in you to play again, in everything you do. Often when I find myself starting to overuse the word *work* in my writings, I put a slash next to it and follow it with the word *play*. Work is really adult play, but we forget this and treat our work as something stressful and serious.

Now that we have set the mood, we can begin our play, our cosmic dance, our work, with the angels.

Communicating with the Angels

Angels take root in our consciousness the moment we establish a connection. Since we have guardian angels who have always been with us, in essence we have always been connected to the angels, especially in our hearts and souls. Angel consciousness is something more; it begins when we become fully aware of the angels around us and the possibilities and wonders they bring to our lives. Establishing a personal connection with the angels is a simple process. You don't even have to say you believe in angels. Just by allowing yourself to be open to the ways of the angels, you will notice all the wonderful happenings the angels promote around you. Then you won't need to believe; you will simply know.

After you have become angel conscious, you will want to communicate with the angels in your own special way. Some people simply converse with the angels as if they were sitting in the room with a friend. Others write letters to the angels. When the angels communicate with us, they do it mostly through inspiration and little signs. They may bring us humor in a dark moment. Or they may help us notice a wonderful coincidence — a synchronism — to let us know all is well.

If you are trying to get angels to prove they exist by speaking to you with a list of reasons you should believe in them, then you are approaching the whole situation with an underlying sense of doubt, and doubt is most likely what you will end up with. All will not be lost, though; the angels can still get through to your heart.

Whereas channeled entities often speak through the medium of words, the angels' language is primarily one of symbols, colors, sounds, and feelings. While they may, on certain occasions, communicate with us in words — perhaps through a voice we may hear, or by leading us to books or films that are especially relevant at a particular moment in our lives — we also receive the angels' messages through various nonlogical, nonlinear conduits, such as dreams, synchronisms, and intuitive flashes, fantasies, and other vague and often "inexplicable" experiences. Angels are like thoughts; they inspire us by instilling ideas into our thought processes and patterns.

Because we are all unique beings, we express our connection to the angels in unique ways. To create a great relationship with your own guardian angel, and any other angel for that matter, you need to create a fertile and rich inner life. Creating an inner life is easy for some and more difficult for others. Some of us may spend too much time dwelling on the issues in our inner lives, while others of us run around never stopping to hear our inner voices. Each of us has an inner life; it is a matter of paying attention to it and giving it strength.

Keeping an Angel Journal

I want to go on living even after my death!
And therefore I am grateful to God for giving me this gift,
this possibility of developing myself, and of writing,
of expressing all that is within me.

— ANNE FRANK

Our consciousness is far more than our waking, physical response. We hear, see, feel, absorb, and record much more information than we are actually aware of. In our dreams we go into a whole other realm, in which the physical body is asleep but our consciousness is experiencing a myriad of sensations. Our waking decisions may seem to be very linear, logical expressions we put forth, yet we are really guided by a higher point of reference that knows the future, the present, and the past, so our actual decisions and responses to life often have very little to do with our narrowly focused logic. We have all looked back on circumstances in our lives and seen how they evolved in an orchestrated way that had very little to do with what we thought we were creating or deciding. This is what is so exciting about having a spiritual response to life with the angels as our companions and cocreators. When we keep track of our lives in a journal, we witness miracles that we might otherwise have missed.

Writing makes a map, and there is something about a journey that begs to have its passage marked.

— CHRISTINA BALDWIN, *LIFE'S COMPANION*

Each of our lives is a special journey of healing, questioning, learning, loving, creating, knowing ourselves, and making peace with ourselves. A journey denotes travel from one place to another. Our lives are pathways, spiritual journeys we embark upon. We do our spiritual traveling in our minds and hearts; we may never leave our homes, but we can still travel very far on our paths. It takes practice, desire, plus courage to venture into the unknown parts of ourselves. Keeping a journal is one of the best ways available for getting in touch with who we are, on all the many levels where we exist and respond. Keeping a journal is about discovering the true stories of our lives, and keeping a journal with the angels strengthens our cocreative relationship with them.

Be careful not to approach your angel journal as a writing exercise. If you think and feel and talk, then you can write. Writing is a natural human activity that has been blemished with rules, comparisons, criticisms, and fears. Writing, just like anything artistic, gets better and easier over time, and ends up with more depth the more often you do it.

My favorite way to keep a journal is the old-fashioned way, using a pen and blank book. I like to draw, paste pictures, and have something physical to take with me when I'm out in the world and get inspired. Of course, you can also keep your journal on your computer, or even put your journal on the

Internet, with all the blog (web log) sites available. Keep track of all of the big and little thoughts that come to you concerning angels. Record your dreams, goals, prayers, worries, and anything else you find lingering in your mind. Mark all of these in your journal; they may provide a needed clue or message later.

Creating an Angel Altar

It's so important to unclutter the mind. For me, creativity is greatly impeded just by the chatter and visual clutter of life. It's really important to have a space that is really clear for whatever is emerging to come.

— ALICE WALKER

An altar is a sacred space of spiritual focus. Altars in churches are tables where offerings are made to God, such as the bread and wine of communion. Most likely you have an altar, and it probably has an angel on it. If not, you need one. Your angel altar doesn't have to be obvious to anyone but you. Find a small table, an area in a bookcase, or a space on top of a dresser; even a windowsill will work. Items on my altars (I have a few of them) include a beautiful cloth, small statues, candles, flowers, prayer beads, crystals, rocks, shells, angel gifts people have given me, incense burners, and turtles — I seem to collect them without really trying.

When you have created an altar, it is a sacred reflection of you. Take time to be in the beauty you have created. Light a candle. Candles illuminate and purify the etheric atmosphere and attract angels. Put on some inspiring music, and ask the angels to join you in the golden love light. Your altar is the perfect place to go when you want to meditate, journal, or engage in any active practice with the angels.

Consider your altar sacred space and private only to you. It's okay to create privacy. This means you can have private thoughts that no one else needs to know or hear, private activities that only you know about, and private feelings you choose to keep inside. Even if you want to have a private lifestyle that you share with only a few people — this is all okay!

I used to think that I was not supposed to keep anything to myself, including thoughts, feelings, or activities I was pursuing. When I kept them to myself, I felt guilty and uncomfortable about it. I guess I thought that being honest meant being candid all of the time about everything. Then I realized that it was okay to be a private person. I gave myself permission to choose who needs to know what and when. Some people have grown up in environments where they had no privacy, and now they either become too private — even to the point of being isolated and secluded — or they simply don't know how to create the privacy they need in their adult lives or don't think it is okay to create it.

Think about your own issues of privacy and how you can create a level of privacy that feels appropriate in your own life. It is up to you to decide how personal you want to be with other people. There are different levels of relating within each friendship, and each friendship or relationship you have is unique. You always have the right to protect your own mental health. If you want to keep things from people, that is your business; you are not violating anyone's right to know, because there is no such thing. There are no rules in the universe that say in order to be a good friend and a good person you have to live a totally open life, available to spill your guts to anyone who might come along. The angels are always available to help protect your inner sanctum. Ask them for deep wisdom in these matters, and you will be "unto yourself" yet available to the world.

Your creativity offers a wonderful arena for expressing private thoughts, feelings, and experiences. You can paint a picture with a certain meaning, and no one needs to know except you. You can write a cryptic poem. You can write a novel based on characters that represent a private aspect of yourself. You can write your feelings in your journal using a secret code, or you can write about yourself in the third person, using a secret code name.

Create a bubble of protection with the angels. When you need sacred space, ask the angels to help you visualize a protective bubble of light around you. The angels will fly around the perimeter of this bubble and ward off any negative influences that would otherwise interfere with your creative energy. They may even intercept phone calls or visits until you are available.

Meditation

That's the arising of something new in humanity. I sometimes call it the unconditioned consciousness. But it is also a field of stillness, where you see the torn roots of the human mind. Once it emerges, it's a process that cannot be reversed. It emerges more and more fully, and you become less and less identified with the structure of thought. And then thought is no longer dysfunctional. It is actually beautiful. It can be used for helpful purposes. It's wonderful — you are no longer looking for an identity in the structure of thought because now you know that who you are is deeper. You are the very awareness prior to thought. You are the stillness that is deeper than thought, much vaster than thought. We call it "stillness," but that's just a word. We've reduced it to something. It's more than that. It's consciousness itself, unconditioned, the essence of each human being.

— ECKHART TOLLE

Meditation, if practiced on a regular basis, is one of the best ways to still the mind and "be here now." Meditation has many benefits, both physical and mental. The words I quoted from Eckhart Tolle sum up the essence of what we can garner from meditating — identifying less with thought and more with stillness. There are many ways to meditate. You can join a group, or sit alone. You can use a mantra or simply pay attention to your breath.

If you have never meditated before, simply sit quietly in a comfortable, peaceful place. Light a candle if you want, and maybe some incense. Then close your eyes and just be. Begin to relax as you breathe. Imagine as you breathe that you are taking in light and it is filling your soul. Mentally ask that your guardian angel be part of your meditation; then let go of mind. Be still. When thoughts come, allow them to come and go without disturbing your inner peace. If you want to use the word *angel* as a mantra, allow the repeating of the word to bring you closer and closer to pure being and inner peace. Meditating for twenty minutes or more brings deep relaxation, and the benefits will show up later in amazing ways. Even one minute of meditation is truly beneficial.

Physiologically, when we meditate, our brain waves slow down and enter the alpha class of brain waves, named *alpha waves* because they were the first electrical activity to be discovered in the brain by Austrian psychiatrist Hans Berger. There are four classes of brain waves. Beta waves operate when we are fully awake and alert. Alpha waves cycle at about half that of beta. Theta is the deep state of tranquility and drowsiness bringing sleep. Then come delta waves, which are the slowest and constitute a deep state of unconsciousness. Hans Berger discovered that alpha waves were rare in anxious people, and if an anxious person did have a few alpha waves, they were smaller than usual (a weaker signal with less amplitude).

So, with all this in mind, we can see that alpha waves are not only natural but a key to getting past anxiety. Learning to drop into an alpha state is a valuable skill for everyone interested in connecting with the angels. In alpha, the mind is open to other forms of communication. Once you start to recognize when your brain is slowing down its cycles, you can take little alpha wave time-outs during the day and ask the angels to help clear the slate and give you a new view of anything you are dealing with.

Angel Mail

Keep on asking and it will be given to you;
keep on seeking and you will find....

— MATTHEW 7:7

Of all the ideas about communicating with angels I have explored, I've found that angel mail is the most popular. It's very effective on many levels.

Angels are special request agents. Special requests cover a wide range of issues, from assistance with immediate tasks, such as finding your lost keys, to help with achieving long-term goals. When we involve angels in our special requests, we are acknowledging the desires of our higher selves. It is fine to ask angels for help with your goals and aspirations. You may think that angels should already know what you want and that you shouldn't ask, but asking is the positive step that sets the action in motion and inscribes it in the divine registry. There is no harm in asking the angels for something, because they only do things for the highest good of all concerned. Prosperity author Catherine Ponder has said, "Your ships come in only after you have sent them out." Asking the angels for a special request is like sending out your ships and asking God to bless them. You are protected from greed by the angels, because they see into excesses and are attuned to your higher consciousness.

With angel mail, you write your special request on a piece of paper and mail it to the angels. The written word is said to have a special power of its own. Declaring your wishes on paper and addressing your letter to the angels is a good way of clarifying your goals and truest desires. To make a special request to the angels, simply take a piece of paper and address it to your own highest angel and the highest angels of the others your request involves. In your request, be specific and define what it is you want as clearly as you can. Always add the phrase "for the highest good of all concerned" to your note. Then express your gratitude. Thank the angels as if the request has already been granted. Also, thank God, and anyone else who has something to do with the request.

A story about one of the Catholic popes describes how he prayed to his guardian angel every day for guidance. When he was scheduled to confer with someone he thought might be troublesome, he would ask his guardian angel to speak with the other person's guardian angel regarding the upcoming meeting. The two guardian angels would work out the disagreements beforehand, and the meeting would proceed without needless arguments.

Apply this idea to angel mail. A problem cannot be solved at the level it was created. If there is someone in your life — your boss, your spouse, your child, your coworker, or your friend — with whom you have trouble communicating without disagreements and arguments over trivial issues, try writing to that person's guardian angel and ask that the situation be understood on the highest level. Then pay attention to what happens the next time you see that person. Look for any subtle or obvious change of heart on the part of that person concerning the areas of disagreement.

You can use this technique whenever you feel resistance from other people. Write to their angels, and state clearly what you want from them, what it is you want them to understand, how you want them to react, and what you want them to do. By writing to a person's guardian angel, you can get past any emotional blocks either or both of you may have in the situation. Use this technique for helping those you care about to do something positive for themselves. If people you know need healing, release, love, or knowledge, write to their highest angels and ask that they be blessed with what they most need. This technique is especially useful if people you know have created situations for themselves that you can't talk about face-to face. Maybe the situation involves something that you can see clearly from the outside but that they are in denial about.

When writing to angels with regard to other people, keep in mind that other people have free will. We experience pain when those we love disappoint us by doing something we don't appreciate. If you have expectations about people, eventually you are going to be disappointed, one way or another. On the other hand, if you don't expect anything and give and release freely, loving unconditionally, you will not allow their negative actions to affect you. If you are trying to influence someone romantically by writing to that person's angel, the best thing to do is to bless and release him or her with love. If you are meant to be with this person, he or she will come to you freely, with no conditions. The angels want you to be happy, but they also know that no other person can make you happy; it's up to you to claim your own happiness first.

When you are ready to "mail" a written request, the first thing to do is to fold and seal it; then find a special place for it. Some people keep their requests in books like the Bible; others use a jewelry box, their wallet, their journal, or their altar. After you mail your request in this way, be prepared for action. You have asked the angels, so listen intuitively for messages regarding your request, or just mail your request and forget about it until it pops into your mind again.

STEPS FOR MAILING REQUESTS TO THE ANGELS

1. Define your request.

2. Write your request on a piece of paper. Specify the angel you are addressing, for example:

"To the guardian angel of _____"
or "To the prosperity brokers" or "To the highest
angel of _____." Somewhere in your
request, include the phrase "for the highest good
of all concerned." Close your request with an
expression of gratitude. "Thank you, God" is
always good.

3. If there are any people who might interfere with
   the fulfillment of your requests, write to their
   guardian angels and ask that anything that might
   block your progress with those people be
   removed.

4. Fold and seal your letter, find a special place for
   it, and consider it mailed.

5. Wait for a response, which may come in the form
   of intuition, opportunities for action, or feelings,
   such as peace of mind and knowing that all is
   well.

Declarations

From time to time, I write out declarations to the angels. I sign
them and put them in a special place, then bring them back out
once in a while to remind me what I have declared. The following are examples I have personally used. Fashion these declarations to your needs, and, of course, feel free to make up
new ones.

The following declaration is for the intention to end negative behaviors.

I, _____, formally and willingly choose and am open to change on an inner level. I would like to eliminate the following behaviors and patterns from my life: [List negative behaviors.]

I agree to take action in the form of [list actions] to help facilitate my progress. I ask the angels to help create a new awareness channel in my mind to alert me to negative patterns when they start so that I can choose a different way of being. I hereby ask the angels to bless this declaration and to instill positive inspiration in place of stale patterns that detract from my happiness.

Thank you, angels, for opening my heart and mind to the glorious beauty of divine love and grace. [It's always a good idea to end by formally thanking the angels.]

The following example is one I use for healing.

Declaration of Health and Well-Being

I, _____, formally and willingly choose to be open to the healing rays of Raphael the Archangel, whose name means Medicine of God.

I ask that the angels under the guidance of Raphael shine the green rays of healing energy upon my being and into the depth of my soul.

I ask that instead of *reacting* with seriousness and fear to the trials of the day, that I begin to *respond* with a sense of humor, inner peace, and hope.

I accept that healing is a matter of balance and centering. I seek to understand and discover the many ways I can balance my life and align my desires with the call of my soul.

I ask Raphael for a heightened appreciation of beauty and its true healing powers. I will allow my inner beauty to radiate out from my soul and embellish all that I do.

I realize and accept the important role I play in the universe right now in helping the angels keep love, light, beauty, and laughter alive on the planet. I agree to help the angels in the following ways: [List the ways.]

I ask for special healing energy to transform the following: [List the areas where you want transformation.]

I thank Raphael and the angels of healing. I thank my guardian angel, and I thank the Higher Power of Abundant Love and Light for the guidance that is always available for my highest good.

This declaration is offered for the highest good of all concerned.

Signed: _____

Date: _____

Calling an Angel Conference

One of my favorite lines from the angel movie *The Bishop's Wife* (the version with Cary Grant), is when the angel and the bishop's wife are taking a cab home and they ask the driver to take the route that goes through a beautiful park. The cab driver then says he likes that — they know where they are going and don't mind taking their time to get there, whereas most people are in a hurry and don't really know where they are going. When you get to a point in your life where things don't seem to be working that well and you feel pressured to accomplish something you have lost sight of, it is time to call a conference and establish an angelic board of directors.

One of the first fun things I started doing when I realized angels were more than cosmic highway patrol officers was to sit down with a piece of paper and call a meeting of my angel council. Napoleon Hill, author of *Think and Grow Rich*, wrote about holding an imaginary council meeting with a group of invisible counselors at night before going to sleep. His council was comprised of nine men whose lifework most impressed him. Hill wanted to become a composite of these men, so in his mind he sat among them and worked on ideas and noble thoughts.

To begin your angel conference, think of goals, dreams, wishes, worries, and anything else that is taking precedence in your consciousness. After identifying the prevailing theme, then you can establish which angels to bring in. You can pick these angels from the ones I described in chapter 1, or you may like to design a special position. I find it works well to bring in God, Jesus, Mary, saints, gods, goddesses, ancestors, gurus, and so forth — any entity or consciousness that you currently resonate to. The next step is up to you. You can do this all in your mind, or you can create a chart or mandala on a piece of paper. Write down a goal for a specific area in your life, and then assign an angel. You can make little drawings or symbols to represent the various parts of your conference. Sometimes I draw circles with the goals or intentions inside, then connect all of them with a line. I usually include a circle of noninterference, and in it write things that interfere with my progress or the names of people I need to transform my interactions with or keep away.

The next step is to imagine the conference. Ask questions, and listen for answers. Write down any insights and new information coming to you. If you are familiar with business meetings, take some of that information and use it as an angel conference formula. There are no rules for the angel conference, so do it your way. Here are some ideas for holding an angel conference:

- Bring a sense of humor and lightheartedness to the table.

- Include candles, flowers, incense, or angel statues; you can bring to the table anything you might find on your altar.

- It's inspiring to put on background music that is uplifting, such as harp or flute music.

- You might want to pick an ANGEL® Card for each issue you are dealing with.

- It is fun to do angel conferences with a close friend or a small group. My friend Shannon and I used to do them together; we would get a poster board and write whatever we needed to on it, and draw pictures, diagrams, and so forth. As the saying goes, "Where two or more are gathered..."

- Feel confident that you know where you are going and have all the time you need to explore your surroundings and smell the roses on the way.

- Basically, remember to have fun, and end with a prayer of thanksgiving.

Bedtime Angel Review

Once asleep man has no real freedom of choice. His entire slumber is dominated by his last waking concept of self. It follows, therefore, that he should always assume the feeling of accomplishment and satisfaction before he retires in sleep.

— NEVILLE

One time when I was babysitting and it was bedtime for my three-year-old niece, she kept getting back up with reasons she didn't need to go to sleep yet. The reasons were very cute, but when I was about to lose my patience, she told me not to worry about how late she was staying up because when she finally went to bed she would go to sleep with two angels. I asked her about the two angels, and she explained that they fly all around her bed, keeping the monsters and ghosts away from her so that she can get a good night's sleep. That excuse worked, and I let her stay up until *she* was ready for bed.

Sometimes our days are filled with monsters in the form of worries, stress, hostile people, and work deadlines. When we go to sleep still carrying these monsters, dreamtime can prove to be a battleground. Humans need sleep because of gravity. We have a constant force field keeping us from floating off the planet, and just by standing up we are working against this force. We need sleep to recover from the day's gravity and seriousness. Thus, it is of the utmost importance that we allow our sleep time to be as calming as possible. If we review our day with the angels before we sleep, the process of resolving our worries works more efficiently. Dreamtime becomes more creative, brilliant ideas come to us, and dreams are more pleasant. (Some people actually do their best thinking in their sleep!)

Reserve some time before you go to sleep for a review of your day. Go over what worked and what didn't. If you are still holding on to worries and disappointments from the day, ask the angels to release them for you. Ask the angels for the chance to work things out in your dreams creatively. After you've gone through the gravity checklist — that is, your seriousness review of the day — switch your focus to the positive and give thanks for the blessings in your life. Think of things that happened during the day that were humorous and meaningful. Ask the angels to keep you in a sweet and light state when you fall asleep. Ask them to keep your dreams sweet and peaceful — taking you with them to the plane of heaven.

If you are worried about the upcoming day, try this technique: Take a piece of paper and write about the upcoming day as if it has already happened. Here's an example.

This morning I woke up fresh and alert at 7:00 a.m., which gave me plenty of time to enjoy my morning coffee and think peacefully about my life. At 9:00 a.m., I left the house; the traffic was smooth, with every car in synch. I found the perfect parking place, and I even got to work early. At 10:00 a.m., my meeting with _____ went perfectly, and she agreed to _____. During lunch, I had more than enough time to take care of some errands, to eat, and to socialize. The rest of the day was very productive and creative. My drive home was wonderful, and dinner with _____ was incredibly romantic and sweet.

I hope you get the idea. When your script is done, ask the angels to bless it. Then, at the end of your "perfect" day, go over your list and see how well you did. This is a good technique to use when you have an important day coming up and you want some unseen help with it.

And, of course, you can also create the next day by visualizing how it will go. This involves visualizing the day in your mind. As you do this, ask the angels for insight into the people you'll be seeing. What are they really like? Is there common ground between you? What are their deepest desires? Ask the angels what phone calls you need to make, and how you can manage and remember the big and little details that so often elude us and end up causing us more work in the long run.

When I create my day, and out of nowhere, little things happen that are so unexplainable, I know that they are the process or the result of my creation. And the more I do that, the more I build a neural net, in my brain, that I accept that that's possible. This gives me the power and the incentive to do it the next day.

— JOE DISPENZA

This technique works because you have loaded your unconscious mind with a program to follow. Our unconscious mind can follow time schedules quite well. Think of a home office that exists in your mind, taking care of the little details while you are out promoting yourself in the world.

Many people watch the news or a violent and stressful show on television right before going to sleep. News is rarely edifying and usually leaves us with a feeling of fear and discomfort, as does a show with violent images and messages. This is not a good way to fall asleep. Reading something inspiring and listening to relaxing music are good alternatives to the violence and degradation of late-night television. If you feel you must watch TV before you go to bed, at least pick something humorous and light — if you can find it.

At bedtime, clear your mind and gather the angels around you, so that you can go to sleep in a higher state of consciousness. When you are no longer worried about the day you just had and you've planned the upcoming day, cultivate a time of peaceful silence and fall asleep. Imagine the angels putting you to sleep, covering you with a warm, cozy blanket of golden love light, and flying around you all night, keeping away the monsters and ghosts and sprinkling gold dust on your hopes and dreams.

Dreamtime

We are so captivated by and entangled in our subjective consciousness that we have forgotten the age-old fact that God speaks chiefly through dreams and visions.

— C. G. JUNG

Our spiritual lives don't stop when we go to sleep; they flourish and nourish themselves. Dreamtime is spirit time and offers a great opportunity to play with the angels. Many artists find that they are given direct inspiration for their art through their dreams. I knew a musician when we were both in high school who had dreams of sheet music written out. He would wake up and write down the notes and then incorporate them into a song the next day. Dreams give us insight into our life journeys, guiding and pointing us in the direction of our true inner selves and toward whatever we need to look at, resolve, create, or transmute.

Dreams are a good way to realize that we are not in control and that this is okay! When you fall asleep, you enter a world where you are at the mercy of your unconscious mind. If you have had trouble with the issue of surrender in your waking life, remember that each time you sleep you have truly surrendered.

SPIRITUAL SLEEP IDEAS

1. Have a favorite scent nearby to sniff when you sleep. Make sure there is fresh air in your bedroom.

2. Visualize a door to the angelic realm, and as you fall asleep imagine it opening and allowing passage for you and the angels to play.

3. Listen to a guided meditation or soothing music as you journey into dreamland.

4. Avoid watching world or local news on television right before bedtime, as this tends to disturb your sleep time.

5. Right before going to sleep, softly focus on a creative project you are involved in. Perhaps write about your goals, visions, hopes, and so forth. Then ask the angels to bring you insight and inspiration for your project during dreamtime. In the morning, write about your project again, especially if you can recall a dream concerning it.

6. Play with creative ways to sleep spiritually. The angels are near when you go to sleep. They can help you clear the day's troubles away and give you a warm, tingling feeling as you float away softly into angelic dreamland.

7. As for dream interpretation, you are the best interpreter of your own dreams. Don't put too much stock in dream-dictionary definitions. Allow the angels to help you interpret your dreams.

Restoring Balance

At its essence, a ritual is something done to restore balance. The changing nature of life itself demands that we seek balance. Balance may not be our actual goal, since things change so quickly, but coming back to a sense of balance is very important in the realization of our goals. All of the practices in this chapter offer ways to restore balance, with the angels as our guides.

Most of us perform little rituals throughout our day without realizing it. Using rituals we can register and honor changes we are willing to make. Remember that the changels are around at all times to guide us in the art of restoring balance. When we do a practice from this chapter, we are registering a spiritual goal with the angels. The angels as our spiritual guardians work on the inner planes while we work on the physical plane to restore balance and give us a sense of spiritual direction.

Ritual is one of those words that some people react to

quite strongly. We do not honor rituals or rites as our ances-tors did, and often things we have not experienced seem threatening to us. This is changing; people are looking for meaning in their lives and for a balance between the sacred and the profane, so they are restoring ritual to its rightful place.

Think about your day. You wake up, and I bet you do pretty much the same thing each morning. And when you are not able to do it, you may feel a bit off. Children naturally per-form little rituals when they are left to play freely. Years ago, I was the guardian of an afternoon day care center and loved to watch as the children would play uninterrupted. Often they would reenact very mythic themes with little rituals using berries, feathers, branches, and whatever else was on hand. Very likely you played this way as a child. We are mythically inclined. If we don't let it out in play or art, we exercise it by watching soap operas and obnoxious talk shows where people live out mythic themes of betrayal, competition, and so-called destined love.

Some people are afraid of performing rituals because they think they might do something wrong. Others may feel that only a priest or member of the clergy can conduct a ritual. We call it *sorcery* when people use rituals to create an imbalance in the doer's favor. The writer Manly P. Hall notes that a "sor-cerer is a person who attempts by some special art to divert the forces of nature to his own personal ends. The true purpose of metaphysics is to perfect the inner self in wisdom, virtue and understanding. All forced growth is sorcery." Forcing our will is not what angel consciousness is about. Acknowledge God, the highest divine light in the universe, and the angels of God; speak from your heart, and correct action will take place with any ritual you set out to do.

When your angel consciousness has become fully integrated and you have nurtured a foundation of confidence, you will be on call for the angels. Often, they will call for you to restore balance, and you will need to perform a ritual. Approach this with an open mind, and allow the angels' "guide-dance" to lead the way.

I mention my friend Jai a lot when I write. One main reason is that besides being a lot of fun, she lives an inner-directed life, on call for the angels, so many great stories come from her. She also is not afraid to create ritual naturally to restore balance in situations. A good friend of Jai's, Sally, died a few years ago, and Sally's mother sent Jai a beautiful little silver jar of some of Sally's ashes. I was visiting Jai at the time, and she said she wanted to do something special to honor Sally and scatter her ashes in a place she loved, but she didn't have any idea what to do. I suggested we go up to the top of a beautiful mountain that overlooks a valley and let the angels guide us in what to do. So we gathered some necessary items — a candle, some incense, a bottle of red wine, Jai's flute — and went off to our designated spot, gathering wildflowers along the way. We came to a little bench and set up our sacred space by lighting the candle, placing the flowers around, and so on. Then I sat in meditation while Jai played her flute.

When Jai was ready, she walked to the edge of the hill and began to free the ashes. A gentle but firm breeze was blowing, the sun was playing games with the clouds, and as the ashes were scattered the lighter ones caught the breeze and made a beautiful exit upward, catching the sunlight; the heavier ones landed quietly on the earth. This is symbolic of us; we are spirit moving upward, and we are human made from the earth. I started singing to God as the ashes went out to help the spirit find its way home. After this we opened our wine and toasted Sally. Then we toasted the Divine Mother who gave us the wine. By being prepared with a few necessities, and letting our intentions and the angels lead us, we spontaneously created a beautiful ritual that helped restore the balance of death and life.

Don't take it too seriously, but remember if you are here helping the angels — and I can say that you most likely are or you wouldn't be reading this book — then it makes sense to open your heart to the divine beat of the universe and engage in ritual. Let go of any need to control, let go of any personal intention of gain, and you will do the right thing.

Mary Poppins had a magical bag she carried to restore balance. So for your work as an angel on call, you might want to prepare your own magical bag with the following:

- It's always wise to include a prayer of correct intention, asking that the angels be strongly present.

- Look around. If there are people acting chaotically, you can change the chemistry of the situation by becoming very peaceful and acutely aware of what can be done to restore balance.

- Creating an altar is a natural response to any dire situation. We see this all the time. Sometimes people put candles or flowers at places where accidents have taken lives. You may be the one to initiate this, so look for flowers, rocks, berries, and anything else that inspires you, and create a space for spiritual focus.

- Angels on call may simply need to smile at a stranger or extend a kindness for balance to be restored.

- Once again, a sense of humor will keep all of this in divine perspective.

Registering Divine Essence

One aspect of ritual means we are registering something in our consciousness that will become an integral part of our evolving spiritual insight. Some meanings of the word *register* are to record, enter, inscribe, list, chronicle, archive, show, manifest, evince. For example, in our letters to the angels, we are registering our heartfelt intentions in the divine registry. Writing in our journals also registers who we are.

In registering our intentions, it is good to examine what is motivating us. We may want a quick fix: to put a little sugar on top, paint over the flaws, win friends and manipulate people, build a house overnight with inferior materials — all of it so that we can slide by to the next day and possibly end up with some money or power to show for it. The quick-fix trend is now so blatant that commercials come right out and portray empty people trying to manipulate and gain control without anything real to back them up. We have lost the essence of character in our society. We have become unreal, unable to express our true selves because we aren't even sure what that means. Too often we seek shortcuts to some utopia we've fantasized about in our minds. We end up blocking ourselves from seeing what is right in front of us, demanding our attention.

I have to admit that when I first started having fun with

the angels, I tended to view the angels themselves as shortcuts around pain and problems — as a force I could depend on to "make it all better." Well, I was partly right. The angels are a force to depend on, but they *don't* make it all better; rather, they help guide us to use our own ingenuity in resolving our problems. There aren't any shortcuts around pain. There are no quick fixes. Eventually the piper has to be paid, but the angels can help us get beyond just wanting the pain gone. They can help us change our perceptions of problems and pain, so that our internal chemistry shifts to a much lighter state.

Here are some things you might want to register with the angels.

- Goals
- Dreams
- Daydreams
- Images
- Creative ideas
- Noble thoughts
- Raves and rants (as long as you don't take them seriously)
- Your gratitude

And here are some ways you can go about registering these things with the angels.

- Prayer
- Song

- Dance

- Painting

- Walking

- Writing

- Nonsense poetry

- Meditation/contemplation

- Building a shrine or altar

- Trance-inducing practices, such as improvising music, gospel singing, or drumming — these are ways of saying, "Yes, God, I will get out of the way, and let your will be done."

Be creative and explore the full range of creative practices and rituals that will nurture your connection with the angels.

CHAPTER FIVE

Awakening Your Prayer Voice

☆   ☆

*Anyone who is too busy to pray
is too busy.*

A prayer is an expression of thoughts, hopes, and needs, an earnest appeal, a solemn request, or a gesture of thanksgiving directed to God or a deity. Prayer is an important component of all religions and takes on different forms, but it is always prayer. We could say that prayer has its own "Buddha nature." Prayer has become popular, and this fact possesses a miraculous magnitude — a power of transformation so great that it is difficult to conceive how crucially important it really is. Combine this with the fact that angel consciousness has touched the lives of many, and we have the true ingredients to create a positive transformation of the planet.

Although our prayers do not go directly to the angels, the angels can serve as our prayer partners; they can listen to our prayer, and help expedite our hearts' requests. Prayer is how we talk to the higher power in our lives. I always address God, the Highest Light in the Universe, the Creator, or the Great Spirit when I pray. The most important truth in prayer is that we are communicating with the highest, most powerful energy in the universe. It doesn't matter if you believe that God is a leaf on a tree or the brightest star in the night, I will respect and honor your belief.

As the Buddhist saying goes, "The one moon shows in every pool — in every pool the one moon." I hope we are all at a point now where when we see the word *God*, we understand that the One God — the ultimate source of divine love and energy — shines in the heart of every person regardless of race, religion, location, or station in life. The Light doesn't change with the name or the rituals — the Light is the Light is the Light. Does sunlight change when it falls upon different faces? The sun remains the same; we are the receivers of its light, and we each have our own ways of facing its light.

There is no power greater than God. "In the beginning was the Word, and the Word was with God, and the Word was God" (John 1:1). The Word is the sound — the vibration from which all things are created, the divine mantra. The sound is the womb of Mother Earth. Take a moment and think about the idea that we come from a vibration — a divine sound. Close your eyes and listen for the sound of God. As you renew yourself with the harmonious tones of the universe, begin to find God within you. Where is your connecting point — your heart, your mind? This will be personal to you. You may feel God in your heart, or as a field of energy encompassing you — the God Within. When we allow God energy to interplay within our beings, we establish alignment with our spiritual centers and the angels. God is in all of us; there are always divine sparks within us that connect us to the flame of humanity, sparks the angels exist to guard.

Now let us shift gears and consider God the infinite — the Above, the Transcendent Force — whose beauty inspires us to cry out to the sky and sing praises with the angels. Think about the expansiveness of the universe. Think about the magnificent force of beauty when the clouds join the setting sun in a symphony of color. Imagine yourself on the highest mountaintop overlooking a sea of humanity. Feel the aching in your heart to fly with the angels into the ether, up through the majestic clouds, and begin to feel the idea of God as the Universe — the Perfect Universe, which provides exactly what we need and gifts us with unlimited possibilities to create and to be love.

Our personal center of God may change depending on our life experiences and feelings in the moment. For example, when you are feeling like a tiny drop in the ocean, in awe of the incredible idea of how little importance a human life can seem to have, then you may want to cry out to God the expansive and ask that God bring the energy within you to remind you that no matter how many humans there are on the earth, each life is a miracle of importance. Each of us has a guardian angel, and our angels whisper in our ears to pay loving attention to God. This keeps us moving toward God, and leads us to a sense of completeness within ourselves. When we pay attention to God, our lives have profound purpose and meaning. We receive a deep experience of the Divine wherever we go in the world.

All Things Are Possible with God

For with God nothing is ever impossible, and no word from God shall be without power or impossible of fulfillment.

— LUKE 1:37

In the Bible it is written that "with God all things are possible." The archangel Gabriel told this to Mary when she could not believe that she would conceive a son with the Holy Spirit. Each of us is part of these possibilities, and the choices we make create the big picture. We can choose to create many wonderful miracles that will make the world better, and give us grace beyond comparison. But because *all* things are possible, this means that choices can be made to ruin things too. There is no power greater than God. God operates within the natural laws of spirit; if we go against God, just think of what we are taking on. Creativity and creation are the ultimate rules. If we end up destroying ourselves as a planet and find that we are a mass of spirits left without a home, that mass mixed in with love will create a new place for us to create more love.

Your heart knows that with God all things are possible. Instead of trying to believe this and intellectualize the possibilities, just know it deeply. Let your knowing run like a fresh mountain stream, bubbling up from the source, always moving. Remind yourself daily. There are various ways to think about this powerful, awesome idea — that with God all things are possible. At times when you pray to God and find that your faith seems to be wavering, just remember that God knows the language of your heart. Our minds, our intellects, and what we see with our eyes are but a tiny fraction of what surrounds us. Sometimes when we pray for help, we begin by doing battle with our intellectual minds, which want to know all the hows and whys. Faith comes with practice and from knowing that the imagination of God is way beyond anything that our minds can perceive or control.

Often when we are stuck in the throes of something uncomfortable, such as our pain, we forget that everything in life can change in an instant. I do not need to remind you how fragile human life is. Know God now, while you are here. Understand that you are free to have your own special relationship with the Divine. You weren't sent to earth with all the rules clearly defined, all the answers laid out, or all of the steps linear. You were sent to earth with definite gifts and abilities — the most important one being your ability to receive and share love. You are a possibility of God, and you entertain God when you "follow your bliss" and free your spirit to be true to yourself.

In the wide range of human experiences and emotions, sometimes God feels very much within us and at other times out beyond our reach — but always there and present for us to send prayers to. Having a foundation made of God means that when we fall down, when we hit the bottom, we fall into the arms of God's angels. If the foundation of our lives is spiritual, we walk on the temple floor in our daily lives. Now, if we don't have a foundation in God, falling may mean we land in the swamp waters of the wasteland. This is where many people either drown or surrender to God.

Prayer Basics

I would love to give you a perfect definition of prayer, one that would make so much sense that everyone who read it would immediately put the book down and begin to pray. I won't be able to do that because prayer is so personal and resides in the nonrational realm. It is also a subject that can present problems. People who don't pray get very nervous when asked about prayer. Some people think we need a strong "religious" foundation to pray, and if they don't have one they may think they should not pray. There are also people who seem to fear prayer because they fear God.

I was taught to pray at a very young age, although I don't remember how it was presented to me. At that young age, I remember knowing God was everywhere. I would talk to God the same way I would talk to a tree or rosebush. I remember times when I felt so much love wash over me from God that my heart took up the entire backyard of my house. It seemed to me then, as it seems to me now, that prayer is a natural part of life, just as natural as our ability to walk, talk, and think.

F. Forrester Church talks about three kinds of prayer in his book *Entertaining Angels: A Guide to Heaven.* The first kind of prayer is confession, through which we make peace with the enemy within us. The second kind of prayer links self to others; this happens when we ask for blessings for others and for situations we want. The third kind of prayer involves saying yes to life and giving ourselves over to God; this is how we express gratitude and trust in the universe.

I like to think of prayer as the way we put ourselves and our paths on the spiritual map. Imagine that each person who prays is like a light on the earth, shining like a star in the night. Light attracts light, so by praying and putting ourselves on the universal spiritual map, we are attracting God in the sweetest way. You have a compass within your soul that always points you magnetically toward your destiny and toward God. Prayer is one of the ways we get in touch with the messages of our souls, for when we pray we utter our truths.

Praying is making a sound unto the Lord, but it does not necessarily mean we make a vocal noise. It means that we send out vibrations of our inner light via our *prayer voice.* We begin feeling comfortable with prayer when we find our prayer voice. This voice is a part of all of us, even if we haven't yet acknowledged it. For people who have been praying for most of their lives, this voice is a familiar aspect of themselves. Take time to know the voice that prays and connects your light to the Divine Source. Let it have its say; let it find a home in your consciousness. Let it emerge gently and try not to direct it; allow it time to unfold in grace. Ask the angels to help you know this voice, which comes from the depths of your being, from seeds of light in your soul.

Praying is often a silent activity, but prayers can also be sung, cried out loud, spoken, or said together with a group. Prayers can be written as declarations, poems, or requests. Prayers can be visualized, made into art, or acted out in rituals. Prayers often take the form of a confession, a moment of truth, a giving over to the Divine. There are many ways, and many reasons, to pray. You are free to have fun with prayer, especially with the angels as your prayer partners. Praying can be a time of humor and joy. Praying can be a serious, solemn event, a time to be with pain and allow a transformation. As humans, we have a range of experiences, and praying is a time to honor what we are feeling and experiencing.

Prayer is a vital part of an imaginative, creative, and heart-centered relationship with the angels. Prayer affects us deeply, and knowing this opens up a new door in our imaginations. The most interesting fact about prayer is that it is a very practical thing to do. Prayer is actually therapy. When you pray, you are engaging a psychic process of healing, which translates into action and exercising the skills to solve problems with your inner wisdom. You are also programming your mind to look for positive solutions and to calm down and respond wisely to life instead of overreacting to situations. Prayer provides a love link to heaven. By praying for guidance, you become an active player in your destiny, without making such a big deal out of understanding it or controlling it. When we talk to God, we talk to our souls. We come to learn how we are forever interconnected to the source of all life.

What is the highest and best way to pray? If I were to answer this, I would be acting as an authority on prayer and I am not. I am simply someone who, for every moment I have spent on earth, has understood how important prayer is and how ultimately loving God is. I can say that the more we pray, the less we grovel or beg for things. Oftentimes we start out praying as if we were children pleading with our parents. We then come to a point where we cocreate our lives and become active players in our prayer outcomes.

So why take the time to pray? To ease our conscience in a situation we feel uncomfortable with? Because we might earn brownie points in heaven? Because we don't want to be personally involved in a situation, so we turn it over to God? Because we really want something? Because we are in trouble and need spiritual help? With regard to these questions, we don't really need to know absolutely why we pray, because the reasons are probably multidimensional and changeable due to the situations at hand. It is best to make prayer a part of your life without having to analyze it too much, or worry too much about the mechanics. Let prayer be a truly spontaneous response to life, no matter how you feel or where you are at. Just be real with God and the angels, and then communicate from that space. As the theologian Matthew Fox relates in his book about prayer, *On Becoming a Musical Mystical Bear*, "A response is spontaneous (from the Latin *sponte*, of one's own will): it is free, it is mine. We respond *because we feel like it*...it is simply an utterance of one's deep feelings." By responding to God, we instantly upgrade ourselves to a higher vibration, regardless of the whys and hows.

When we pray, we are actually seeking divine wisdom, regardless of what our words or intentions may indicate. Wisdom is not easy to define, and it is not easy to find great examples of wisdom right now. I think if we go looking for wisdom in all the usual places — TV, politics, group mentality, leaders, economics, and so on — we will probably find a lack of wisdom rather than good examples. What constitutes a wise person? As I envision wisdom, there are some definite indicators. For one, I am always alerted to wisdom in people when they can admit that they were wrong, or that their thoughts and beliefs have changed. I am repelled when I see people hanging on and defending worn-out beliefs just because they're afraid they might look bad if they admitted changing. So wise people are not always concerned with appearances or with what others may think; they act on their truths.

Here are some of my inner knowings about prayer.

- To pray means to communicate with the very heart and soul of our universe.

- Praying is a way to tap into the source of all pure love.

- A prayer is spiritual fuel. It is light. It guides us to understand the Christ consciousness.

- Prayer is a renewal of faith, inspiration, and meaning.

- Prayer is an offering of love that engages our highest level of being.

- Prayer allows us to listen to the voice within, to our deepest honesty.

- Praying gives us the chance to step aside from our seats of control and witness Divine Providence in action.

- God knows what our goals are, and we short-change ourselves when we fixate only on goals.

Pray to be filled with divine inspiration to carry you to your goals.

Here are four basic ingredients for prayer.

1. GREET: As in "Dear God and your loving angels," "Mother, Father, God," "Great Spirit."
2. PRAISE: "You are most holy." "Hallowed be thy name." "Hail Mary, full of grace."
3. REQUEST: State the basis of your prayer.
4. THANK: "Thank you, God."

Here are some places to pray.

- Anywhere and everywhere.
- In your home.
- In your car.
- With others.
- In a park.
- In a church.
- Most of all, prayer takes place in the temple of your mind.

Here are some times to pray.

- Pray consciously to change a situation.
- Pray when you are feeling intense fear.
- Pray when you are feeling joy and thanksgiving.
- Pray when you fear for others.

- Pray when you know you need a change in your life.

- Pray without ceasing.

- Pray as a response to life.

And when it comes to how to pray, just begin and you will know.

Heavenly Direction

Sometimes we get lost and refuse to ask for directions. We all know how things can get worse if we continue traveling in the wrong direction. When we are feeling lost in life, the angels can help point us in the direction we are destined to go. The key is to stop and ask. There is no need to put a value judgment on getting lost; it is actually quite important at times. Getting lost might prove to be the first time we've allowed ourselves to experience humility and become conscious of the ways of angels. We have spiritual help when we need it, want it, and ask for it through prayer.

The angels are natural prayer partners. They love our prayers. Praying makes the angels a true part of our spiritual paths, for they hear our prayers and know what we are asking of God. One important point to remember is that we don't pray *to* angels, yet we can pray *with* angels. Angels can give wings to our prayers; they carry our prayers to God, to the infinite realm where all things are possible. Angels are often the answers to our prayers. A good way to address your angel, if you don't have a particular name, is "Guardian Dear."

Angels are important to prayer. Whether we are conscious

of it or not, they are constantly working for God as they attend to the needs of the prayerful. Regardless of how minor the request may seem to us, it is important in heaven; however, the request has to have a spiritually attuned intent, meaning it vibrates with what heaven has to offer. If we pray for things of the world or ways to manipulate, the angels can't vibrate at such a frequency, and we will not receive their assistance.

Fate

If everything is destined to happen in a certain way, why would we want to bother praying? Who controls our destiny? Do we, or is everything set up beforehand and we just go along, filling in the picture? In many ways these questions can only be answered by God, but that doesn't mean we can't speculate or come up with theories. My theory, or current way of responding to this question, is based on the difference between soul and spirit. When I first became "serious" about my spiritual path, I went in the direction of spirit. I wanted to transcend all things earthly and ego-based. Through meditation, visualization, and prayer, I attempted to rise above myself and connect with the unitive state of the Godhead, or the collective consciousness. I really thought that by doing this I would not have any of the problems and struggles that everyday life brought my way. Life would then be blissful and free from human struggle.

What actually happened was I found new struggles and problems, and they seemed even more crucial because I thought I was doing all the right spiritual things. Instead of feeling lighter, my life was feeling a bit heavier. I kept praying and meditating. As I discussed in the introduction, one day, in a very simple way, without blaring trumpets or fanfare, the angels got a message to me that changed everything. When I came across the saying "Angels can fly because they take themselves lightly," all at once I felt a deep sense of humility, humor, love, joy, and wonder. I feel that our souls anchor us to this life, so to speak. Ironically, the angels, who could be thought of as pure spirit, helped me find my soul and honor the importance of being human. Of course, both spirit *and* soul are significant.

The soul is programmed to experience certain things. This programming could be due to reincarnation, astrology, or the unique experience of our own DNA encoded with messages from our ancestors. The explanation is not the most important thing — just the acknowledgment that your soul holds the key to how you are drawn mysteriously along in life, finding yourself in a great many amazing situations, some of which you are sure you wouldn't have volunteered for.

Spirit represents our free will, the idea that we are not locked into any one particular destiny or way of being. We can lift ourselves out of the "wheel of karma," so to speak. I think our best bet is to realize that too much striving to go beyond our souls, beyond our attachment to life — using our free will to bypass lessons — will create an imbalance. Although we create our own destinies through our choices and attitudes, there are also things we are here to experience. The experiences of our souls are not always charming, and we may wonder why we have to suffer such trials, but in the long run we will take from these experiences some great truths and we will then use our spirits to go in positive directions. Too much spirit brings too much struggle. Too much complacency makes us victims of our souls, of life. As usual we need integration and balance, things we achieve through prayer and awareness.

Each life is like a great adventure. Some lives are like the life of Indiana Jones and others are marked by calmer guideposts, but we are all here on a big adventure. The definition of *adventure* is a risky undertaking, a challenging experience, a quest, an unusual and exciting experience, and an escapade. If fish spend all of their time in the water, would they know that there is anything else? We have all heard the saying "Go with the flow." Well, recently I saw a T-shirt with the saying "Only dead fish go with the flow." So I began exploring the idea that if we always go with the flow, we are like dead fish. Our spirits wither when we just sit back swallowing everything whole, gulping water, getting knocked around by life, going onward to who knows where. Soon after seeing that T-shirt, I went camping near one of the most beautiful streams in the world. I spent some time watching how fish actually go downstream. They don't go with the flow; they dart around, they swim across currents, they explore, and sometimes they swim upstream.

I look back on my life, and at times it appears that something else was making choices for me. I propose that we operate on different levels of our psyches, which are not always in the forefront of our waking consciousness. So one part of our psyche may guide us into situations for our growth, or away from situations that we want that would not be right. I firmly believe that there are certain personal patterns that we are here on earth to change; these patterns may also reflect the collective psyche. I also think that there are ancestral patterns that we have been born into that we alone can change to create a better future. We cannot afford to be dead fish in these matters, because patterns can be difficult to change; they are often strong currents for us to swim against. The most challenging aspect of our great adventure is doing what we came here to do. It is never easy; otherwise this experience of human life would have another purpose. What I mean by this is that if all our problems were solved, we could spend our time on earth doing something else, but right now there are problems to play out. The great gift is that we can experience moments of great enjoyment, ecstasy, and deep love along the way, but only if we are awake and doing our own inner work.

So back to our question: If everything is destined to happen in a certain way, why would we want to bother praying? The answer to every spiritual question, in my opinion, has something to do with love. Love is always our saving grace; it is our true reason to be. So for me, love is the answer.

Transmuting Pain

As we know, growth can be painful, but labor pains bring the joy of birth. When I was about five years old, one of my most earnest prayers was asking God to remove all pain from all people, to protect us from all the things that could hurt us. I was especially concerned with physical pain and was hoping my prayers would lead to a day when my knee wouldn't hurt if I skinned it while riding my bike. I added that it would be good if God could also get rid of all the spiders. My father was listening to my prayers one night and heard me asking this. He gently made me understand how important it is that we feel pain when we get hurt; the pain signals us to tend to our

wounds so they don't get worse. He also said that it was important to feel pain in certain situations so that we wouldn't repeat
them, and he explained to me why spiders were important. I
didn't understand the whole gist of our conversation on pain
when I was five, but it stayed with me, and eventually I understood very well how important pain and spiders are.

Is pain a feeling or the result of a feeling? Is it a message
or a punishment? Whatever pain is, we have a natural tendency to avoid it; this is part of our survival instinct. But when
pain is actually present, the avoidance can cause us a great deal
of trouble. Pain can be monumental, and when it is at its
worst, this is the time to go into the core of the pain and confront it. We can confront emotional and physical pain through
making art out of it or by doing a dialogue with it; our imaginations offer a vast resource of tools we can use to honor
pain. Pain signals the time for constant awareness through
prayer.

About ten years ago, a window fell on my left hand, crush-
ing two of my fingers. This happened on a Saturday morning,
so I knew that my doctor wouldn't be in, and I was strongly
repelled by the idea of an emergency room visit. This "little"
accident happened at a most crucial time. I had papers due for
a class I was taking, a book project to complete, and several
other important tasks. I probably went into a state of shock
from the overwhelming physical pain and the implications of
this injury for my everyday life. So I prayed for help. The next
thing I did was take a shower. I just wanted to be in water.
Then I called a friend and told her what had happened. She
recommended I take Bach Flower Rescue Remedy (which I
really believe in) and also put it on my fingers. After that,
I decided to take a nap.

This posed an interesting problem. I was in so much pain that sleeping seemed impossible, and I had to keep my hand in a certain position or it felt like it would throb right off my arm. What I did next was to quiet my mind, say a prayer, and take myself right into the very source of the pain. This wasn't easy, but I kept at it until I knew I was in complete alignment with the pain coming from the damaged nerves in my fingers. When I reached this point, I fell asleep. Of course I'm not suggesting that everyone follow my course of action. Several of my friends thought I was crazy. When Monday morning came and I went to visit my doctor, he sent me downstairs from his office to get X-rays, and the X-ray technician told my doctor that he had no idea how I had gotten through the weekend without major pain medicine; he wondered who I was because the fracture to my two fingers was so severe that most people would have collapsed.

I am using my story as a metaphor of what we can do with pain. Alchemy happens when we go to the wound for our healing. In my case, the pain subsided enough for me to sleep when I took my point of consciousness to the site of the most intense pain. When we choose to heal — to become whole — we have to bring into view all that we are, and our wounds are a living part of us too. Instead of trying to cut them out and ignore them, ask that they bring insight and teaching. If you are in pain or struggling with something, allow it to evolve by being there. Feelings pass and change. Pray not that the pain cease right away, but that you somehow honor its message the same way you would honor a message from an angel. Pain doesn't last, it is like a forming bud on a fruit tree, and its fragrant blossom is joy. We won't get the fruit if we cut off the bud of pain.

There is instant alchemy in *facing* fear, as opposed to being paralyzed by or avoiding fear. We can start by sharing our fears with God through prayer. We can ask for extra courage in a situation, for the strength and faith to rise above whatever seems threatening to us. This is so simple, but many people can't seem to do it. In the beginning, inner work and facing the unknown parts of ourselves is a little like learning to swim when you are afraid of the water. So approach it gingerly. Get to know the properties of the water before you try to swim in it. Don't go into the basement unless you have built a strong foundation for your house. Our lives need a foundation, and we achieve this when we pray and get to know God and the ways of angels in our own special ways.

Forgiveness via Wisdom

We can forgive even the most horrendous crime against us, and prayer provides the surest avenue for this forgiveness. Forgiveness does not mean you have to forget; the energy is best spent on being willing to forgive and finding compassion in your heart, as opposed to forgetting the wrong. It is not always wise to forget harms, but it is wise not to dwell on them. We can find a way to love the worst of our enemies, and by doing so we release a blast of love so pure into the heart of the world that all over the place lead begins to shine like gold. This transformation doesn't happen without prayer though. We need God's help to love our fellow humans, and to think we can do it alone is pure hubris.

The angels are on hand for transmuting the energy spent holding on to past wrongs. If you are waiting until you perceive the wrongdoer has been punished, you may wait too long, damaging your own psyche in the process. If you are waiting for the wrongdoer to ask you for forgiveness, you may wait forever. The point is you need to do some release work on the issue now. This is tricky territory to navigate — thank God we have our angels to lend a hand. Just keep in mind that by holding on to resentment, you are creating a strong connection and cosmic link to the one person in the universe you most dislike. What if our act of forgiveness is the very thing that can create a change in the other party? What if our holding on to a wrong keeps God from sending out some instant karma?

Sometimes those we love are the hardest to forgive. If you don't know how to forgive, that is okay. The first step is simply being willing to forgive. Then you can use a practice such as writing to the angel of the other person involved. Ask your guardian angel for a new perspective on the situation. Then give the situation the healing power of time, and then even more time, and more forgiveness.

Sometimes we need to forgive ourselves, instead of projecting out onto others. One day while driving my car, I kept noticing things that were wrong with all the other cars on the road. One had a taillight out, one was spewing dark smoke out of its tailpipe, and another had a bad tire. Then I realized that if any of these things were wrong with my car, I wouldn't know it because I was busy driving. I, too, could have a taillight out and not even know about it. We don't have eyes in the back of our heads; we don't "see" ourselves completely. But we can develop awareness and use anything that happens to us and others as great learning experiences. Instead of projecting negative traits onto others, look first inside to see if you have a trace of what you find so awful in others. Ask for an angel view of any situation you get stuck with; then ask the angels for help releasing it from your psyche.

A reader named Nickie V. sent me a letter with the following prayer tool. If you are in a difficult situation with a person, one that seems impossible to heal, in prayer say to the person in question, "The Christ in me greets the Christ in you." Repeat this three times in the morning and evening. I used this tool recently, and my heart has softened and my thoughts have lightened in relation to a difficult issue I had with someone. It may take time, but this practice holds the power of higher change.

Another reader named Jo Ann Murphy sent in a powerful forgiveness prayer she knows to promote quick healing results. The instructions are to say it morning and night for at least ten days.

> Picture the person smiling, and send a stream of light from your heart to the person as you say: "[Person's name], I forgive you for anything you have said or done in thought, word, or deed that has caused me pain in this or any other lifetime. You are free, and I am free. [Person's name], I ask you to forgive me for anything I have ever said or done in thought, word, or deed that has caused you pain in this or any other lifetime. You are free, and I am free. Thank you, God, for giving me the opportunity to forgive [person's name] and myself."

The following loving-kindness meditation is the basis of a Buddhist practice. You can rearrange the words, repeat it many times, or use it as a powerful blessing prayer.

If anyone has hurt me or harmed me,
knowingly or unknowingly,
in thought, word, or deed,
I freely forgive them.
And I too ask forgiveness
if I have hurt anyone or harmed anyone,
knowingly or unknowingly,
in thought, word, or deed.

May I be happy.
May I be peaceful.
May I be free.

May my friends be happy.
May my friends be peaceful.
May my friends be free.

May my enemies be happy.
May my enemies be peaceful.
May my enemies be free.

May all beings be happy.
May all beings be peaceful.
May all beings be free.

Prayers of Our Ancestors

Aspire to be an Ancestor instead of fantasizing about eternal youth. But don't confuse Ancestors with genetic connections or biological offspring. Ancestors sit at the edge of the tribe and protect us from evil spirits: injustice, sham, hypocrisy, exploitation, destruction of the planet. Ancestors come in

*many forms, including individuals and ideas that help the
tribe continue for several generations.*

— JAMES HILLMAN

Do you know how your ancestors prayed? Do you even know
anything about your ancestors? Many of us are missing
the conscious presence of our ancestors in our daily lives. I say
conscious because, recognized or not, they are with us. What
have our ancestors left us with? How do we go about evolving
the patterns set forth in our DNA? Trace part of your ancestry,
and find a prayer or way of worshipping connected with your
ancestry and bring it into your life in a new way.

Many of us grew up hearing certain prayers repeated over
and over throughout our lives. Prayers that get passed down to
us contain powerful words that we often don't look closely at.
I am including a few prayers from my ancestors in this book.
Explore the traditions from your own ancestry or your own
religion (if you have one), and look at them with new eyes.
Start a prayer collection from different religious traditions.
Think about what these prayers really mean and who wrote
them. What do they tell you about the essence of prayer?

AMEN

I was taught to end each prayer by saying, "In Jesus' name,
amen." For years I said this without really thinking about what
it meant. *Amen* means to assent, to express agreement, to con-
sent. Now I understand that when I say the words *In Jesus'
name, amen*, I am agreeing to the highest principle of the
Christ consciousness; I am boosting the strength of my prayer
by agreeing with Christ.

The Lord's Prayer is a prayer said around the world

countless times a day. I use the version from the Amplified Bible. Jesus taught his followers this prayer, and he said: "Your Father knows what you need before you ask Him. Pray therefore like this."

> *Our Father Who is in heaven, hallowed (kept holy) be Your*
> *name.*
> *Your kingdom come, Your will be done on earth as it is in*
> *heaven.*
> *Give us this day our daily bread.*
> *And forgive us our debts, as we also have forgiven (left,*
> *remitted, and let go of the debts, and have given up*
> *resentment against) our debtors.*
> *And lead (bring) us not into temptation, but deliver us from*
> *the evil one. For Yours is the kingdom and the power*
> *and the glory forever. Amen.*

— MATTHEW 6:9–13

DIVINE MOTHER ENERGY

The quintessence of reverence and compassion is the Divine Feminine, the Mother, the feminine face of God that says, "thou mayest" rather than "thou shalt." When you want to be mothered, to feel the true essence of love — the love that has no conditions, no requirements — call upon your Mother in heaven. These prayers to the Blessed Virgin Mary from my ancestors' tradition have been used by countless people in times of severe danger, and countless miracles have ensued.

> *Hail Mary, full of grace, the Lord is with thee.*
> *Blessed are thou among women, and blessed is the fruit of*
> *thy womb, Jesus.*

*Holy Mary, Mother of God, pray for us sinners now and at
the hour of our death.*

*Hail, holy Queen, Mother of Mercy, our life, our sweetness,
and our hope.*
To you do we cry, poor banished children of Eve.
*To you do we send up our sighs, mourning, and weeping in
this vale of tears.*
*Turn, then, O most gracious Advocate, your eyes of mercy
toward us.*
*And after this our exile, show unto us the blessed Fruit of
your womb, Jesus.*
O clement, O loving, O sweet Virgin Mary!

A PRAYER OF ST. FRANCIS OF ASSISI

I have always loved this prayer of the gentle monk Saint Francis of Assisi. This is a powerful prayer that gladly summons the angels, and reminds us of the essence of compassion.

Lord, make me an instrument of your peace.
Where there is hatred, let me sow love.
Where there is injury, pardon;
Where there is doubt, faith;
Where there is despair, hope;
Where there is darkness, light;
Where there is sadness, joy.
O Divine Master, grant that I may not so much seek
To be consoled, as to console,
To be understood, as to understand,
To be loved, as to love,
For it is in giving that we receive;

It is in pardoning that we are pardoned;
It is in dying that we are born to eternal life.

PSALMS

A psalm is a song of praise to the Lord. Psalms have great power and can be used as a daily prayer ritual, for nothing can restore balance like tapping into the ancient laws of God. I often read Psalm 91 at angel gatherings, and one time a woman came up afterward and shared a beautiful story about this psalm. She had come to a very difficult place in her life and was suffering deep depression, so deep that she was thinking about suicide. One day she reached out to her father and told him how depressed she was. He let her know he understood what she was going through and asked her to promise him that before she did anything drastic she would read Psalm 91 every day for a month. This had helped him get through a similar time. She did so, and said that the psalm changed her life miraculously — a case of true alchemy! Many also find Psalm 23 an alchemical prayer.

1   *He who dwells in the secret place of the Most High shall remain stable and fixed under the shadow of the Almighty [whose power no foe can withstand].*

2   *I will say of the Lord, He is my refuge and my fortress, my God, on Him I lean and rely, and in Him I [confidently] trust!*

3   *For [then] He will deliver you from the snare of the fowler and from the deadly pestilence. [Then]*

4   *He will cover you with His pinions, and under His wings shall you trust and find refuge; His truth and His faithfulness are a shield and a buckler. [Then]*

5   *You shall not be afraid of the terror of the night, nor of the arrow [the evil plots and slanders of the wicked] that flies by day,*

6   *Nor of the pestilence that stalks in darkness, nor of the destruction and sudden death that surprise and lay waste at noonday. [Then]*

7   *A thousand may fall at your side, and ten thousand at your right hand, but shall not come near you.*

8   *Only a spectator shall you be [yourself inaccessible in the secret place of the Most High] as you witness the reward of the wicked.*

9   *Because you have made the Lord your refuge, and the Most High your dwelling place, [Verses 1, 14]*

10   *There shall no evil befall you, nor any plague or calamity come near your tent.*

11   *For He will give His angels [especial] charge over you, to accompany and defend and preserve you in all your ways [of obedience and service].*

12   *They shall bear you up on their hands, lest you dash your foot against a stone. [Luke 4:10, 11; Heb. 1:14]*

13   *You shall tread upon the lion and adder, the young lion and the serpent shall you trample under foot. [Luke 10:19]*

14   *Because he has set his love upon Me, therefore will I deliver him; I will set him on high, because he knows and understands My name [has a personal knowledge of My mercy, love and kindness; trusts and relies on Me, knowing I will never forsake him, no, never].*

15   *He shall call upon Me, and I will answer him; I will be with him in trouble, I will deliver him and honor him.*

16   *With long life will I satisfy him, and show him My salvation.*

— PSALMS 91

1   *The Lord is my shepherd [to feed, guide and shield me]; I shall not lack.*

2   *He makes me lie down in [fresh, tender] green pastures; He leads me beside the still and restful waters.*

3   *He refreshes and restores my life — my self; He leads me in the paths of righteousness [uprightness and right standing with Him — not for my earning it, but] for His name's sake.*

4   *Yes, though I walk through the [deep, sunless] valley of the shadow of death, I will fear or dread no evil; for You are with me; Your rod [to protect] and Your staff [to guide], they comfort me.*

5   *You prepare a table before me in the presence of my enemies; You anoint my head with oil; my [brimming] cup runs over.*

6   *Surely only goodness, mercy and unfailing love shall follow me all the days of my life; and through the length of days the house of the Lord [and his presence] shall be my dwelling place.*

— PSALMS 23

Prayer Makes a Difference

The following story can be found on the Internet in slightly different versions, and it is sent around in emails. I love the Internet, and I love email. There is a bit of the game of Telephone involved when we receive circulated emails; the message takes on new forms as it travels. I haven't listened to the tape credited as the original source of this story, but I think the story itself points out some powerful things about prayer and how our reactions and responses to things need to be considered at all times, so I wanted to include a version of it. This story may even be apocryphal, but the message is important in any case.

Carolyn Myss, a well-known medical intuitive, in her Energy Anatomy tape program, recounts the incident of a woman who had been in a car accident. She had a near-death experience. During this experience she found herself hovering over the car. While she was hovering over it, she could hear the responses in the cars backing up behind her. She could hear them saying, "Damn, oh damn, this is just what I need," and other similar comments. Many of the drivers were mad, and cursing her for making them late. She started feeling weaker as a result of what she heard.

Then she saw a ray of light coming from an auto a few cars back, and she zeroed in to hear a woman saying this prayer, "God, if you can, please help this woman."

At this moment, the woman who was in the accident felt herself being drawn back to her body, and heard, "It is not your time..."

But just before returning to her body, she took note of the license plate of the woman in prayer.

When the woman healed, she appeared at the praying woman's door with a bouquet of flowers, and said, "Thank you for your prayers; you saved my life!"

Making Prayer Personal

I once read a magazine article about prayer that included quotations from some prominent authors talking about ways
people may misuse prayer or be "narcissistic" and manipula-
tive in their praying. They were concerned that people would
pray for things they want, or pray "just because it works." This
article upset me. I was glad to see an article on prayer, but I
was concerned that such parameters could keep some people
from praying because they might be afraid of not doing it right
or, worse, might begin to think that they were narcissists if
they asked the Great Creator for something specific. Narcis-
sism is a very drastic accusation. I am not afraid to encourage
people to pray. I am convinced that most people deep inside
want to evolve and be of help to the planet.

Personally, I think the best authority on prayer is our
inner guidance; it's important to remember that when we
pray, God is the force listening. What I mean is that when we ask
God for anything in prayer, whether or not our request is
narcissistic, God remains the same and we will receive what
we need *spiritually* — that is, what is spiritually correct
according to the situation. Each of us has our own special relationship with God, so our prayers are an expression of that
relationship. Keep in mind that no one needs to know about
your prayers and the way you pray unless you want them to.
Jesus said, "And when you pray, go into your most private
room, and closing the door, pray to your Father Who is in
secret; and your Father Who sees in secret will reward you
in the open" (Matthew 6:6). Your own relationship to prayer is
private and personal and doesn't need added worries! Begin to
trust your own inner authority. If your intent is true and pure

when you pray, then your prayers will be like music to God and the angels. Remember that God reads our hearts when we pray, "for the Lord sees not as man sees; for man looks on the outward appearance, but the Lord looks on the heart" (1 Samuel 16:7).

Since there have been some indications that prayer makes a difference in healing and in predicted outcomes, some scientists now want to conduct studies to figure out how and why. Let them have their fun. We don't really need to know exactly how and why prayer works. Our souls know. Our spirits guide us in prayer, and our logical minds are often left confused, but let us give our consciousness a little more credit. We are more than our perceived physical responses to life. We feel, hear, and record so much more information than we are aware of. We may think that everything in our lives is very linear and that we make very logical decisions, but in reality we are guided by a higher point of reference operating in a space that linear time does not touch — the cosmic dance. Make prayer an everyday part of your life; your relationship with the angels will deepen and wisdom will guide your instincts.

CHAPTER SIX

Touched by the Angels

ANGEL POEM

Angels are very holy and they are ten feet tall.
They wear beautiful white dresses and a halo.
They guide you every minute of the day.
Even though you can't see them, they are still here.
And I know you can't put your hand out and touch them.
They make you happy when you are sad.
Angels help and love you very much.
Sometimes in pictures Angels have wings, but I'm not sure
    if they have wings in real life.
They live on the earth with you, except they're still in
    heaven, too.
I know it's confusing to you — it's confusing to me, too!

— ELIZABETH ANN GODFREY (AT AGE EIGHT)

When my first book, *Messengers of Light*, was published, I received a letter from an excited reader before I even had a copy of the book in my hand. Letters came from all over the world, from all kinds of people, from all kinds of places. I shared some of my favorite letters in a book entitled *Answers from the Angels*. In this chapter, I've chosen some of the letters and stories I've received over the years that help to strengthen our understanding about how the angels help us on a personal level. I have also included some writings from, and interviews with, some angel light workers, who have much to teach about art, music, and the devic kingdom, including an interview with musician Carlos Santana.

So many powerful stories exist to help us know the angels by heart. Some of my favorite accounts concern very simple everyday experiences that are touched by angel light and become life-changing miracles. We learn so much from sharing our experiences with one another. That's why the angels bring new friends and people into our lives who become kindred spirits in our journey here on earth.

Tara's Angels

I was preparing to lead a workshop on angels in Los Angeles, when two of the participants immediately caught my eye as they entered the room. I noticed their angel T-shirts — which at that time were rare — but mostly I noticed the extraordinary light they were radiating. I was also struck by the fact that one of them was so young, but so wise looking and spiritually confident. After the workshop they came up to me and handed me a copy of *Messengers of Light*, the first book I wrote.

This copy had developed a personality all its own. It had the flexibility of a well-read book, with little notes to the angels throughout. They asked me to sign it to Tara, the young girl's older sister, who had been killed in a car accident that past August. As I held the book, they told me a few things about Tara and some interesting things she did leading up to her crossing over. The week prior to the accident, she made three ceramic angels at summer camp, one for each member of her family.

Two days before the accident, she gave her younger sister the book I held in my hands and said, "I will always be your guardian angel." The night of the accident, at dinner she asked her mother, "Do you believe that when your work is completed on this plane you go to another plane of existence to do something more meaningful?" Her mother paused, then said yes. The morning after the accident, her family found one angel-shaped cookie on the kitchen counter that Tara had made, and sitting out in her bedroom were lyrics to a song entitled "I'm an Angel."

Hearing this after the workshop was transcendent for me; I can't imagine how I must have seemed to the two of them, but they both had such a wonderful strength and love about them that I mustered up enough strength to sign the book for them. My emotions were swirling beyond tears.

About a week after the workshop, I tried to find a way to reach them. I got a list of the participants, but I couldn't figure out who they were from the list. I had no luck in finding them, so I said a prayer that our paths would cross again. One day a few years later, I was thinking about Tara while I was writing *Angel Wisdom*, a daily meditation book. I thought about her short time here and found myself flooded with emotion. Then an image of a beautiful comet flashed through my mind. I thought about how comets come through so quickly, giving us just enough time to feel the awe of their beauty before they are gone to share the light somewhere else. So I wrote a meditation on this and then sent out a prayer that I learn how her family was doing.

The next day I arrived home to a phone message from an excited friend telling me about an awesome angel store she had been to, and telling me that the store was named after a girl who had died, and that my book had been very important to her. I thanked God right away for answering my prayer.

Later that day, author and producer Rex Hauck called me to discuss a TV project he was doing on angels. He asked me for the names of some people to contact, and before I had even made contact with them, I told him the story of Tara and recommended he call her parents, Kirk and Sandy Moore, right away. He did, and "'Tara's Angels" was the opening story for his prime-time special: *Angels: The Mysterious Messengers.*

Since then, the Moores have done many amazing things. The store has moved into the Center for Universal Truth, which Rev. Sandy Moore and Rev. Kirk Moore cofounded. Kirk has written two books about his experiences, which I highly recommend. I think the most important thing I learned from meeting all of them is that by becoming a unique possibility of God's love, by staying awake and conscious in the midst of deep pain, you create a pattern of healing in the universe that deeply blesses others (contact information for the Moores is in the Resources section at the back of this book).

Stories from Answers from the Angels

The following stories provide a sampling of the multitude of letters I've received over the years from those whose lives have been touched by the angels.

SHANNON, CALIFORNIA

Several years ago I had just come through a long period of depression that resulted in dissolving my marriage of ten years. I guess I hadn't realized the tremendous burdens of the relationship, or its lack of spiritual basis, until it was over, when I experienced a most astonishing renewal of innocence and faith in God. There is nothing to compare with the beautiful gift of innocence. I will be forever grateful and in love with God for the freedom from guilt and the burden of blaming myself. It was during this period that I began to know the presence of angels.

It is difficult to describe the sweetness of the way angels ministered to me then. They were healing my heart with a profound subtlety, and I was blossoming from the inside out with joy and hope for the future; physically, I was beginning to look much younger, and emotionally I was demonstrating stamina unknown to me before.

In my powerful feelings of gratitude, I was moved to pray constantly. But in my spiritual immaturity, I asked for things that were better left unanswered. No matter; I was in such grace during this period that the angels would send me gifts to console me and let me know I was not alone.

On one such occasion, my son Gideon and I were driving down the main street leading to our home. Looking ahead toward the corner where we lived, I saw a flash of gold on the street. It took a few seconds to register in my mind, but then I stopped the car in the middle of the street, just where we turned onto our street. I opened the door and looked down to see — just within my reach without my having to undo my seat belt — a golden angel statue lying on her side. I swept her up, and in my glee I screamed. Gideon was amazed.

We hurried home and rushed into the house to look at her. On close examination, we saw she was carefully sculpted in the repose of prayer (since she is on her knees, the bottoms of her bare feet show delicate and lovely) and hand painted in Italy. She has a golden gown wrapped around her small body. In a word: beautiful.

Since then, my angel experiences are not so materialistically spectacular, but the honeymoon with God I was given during that time changed me and permanently reassured me of the presence of love, goodness, and mercy.

JEFF BOUTEL, WASHINGTON

I've been on a singular, upward path for eighteen years. I am now thirty-six, so that's half my life, which has passed at the speed of light. I am a man compelled — drawn. I have no choice but to seek truth.

At the end of your workshop, when you asked everyone to pick an ANGEL® Card, I picked the card with the word *Grace* on it. I assumed *Grace* referred to God's grace. But two days later, I was awakened by the most compelling thought: Grace is the name of my guardian angel.

The next day, when I went to collect my mail, guess what I found? A postcard with the word *Grace* printed on the front. On the back was a beautiful hand-written love poem, which was signed "Grace." Now the interesting thing is, I have no friends or acquaintances by the name of Grace. In fact, I've never met anyone named Grace — until now. I've no doubt my guardian angel was sending me a very clear message.

CHRISTY SCHAFER, NORTH CAROLINA

Oh, by the way, the day I started asking the angels for guidance, two beautiful poems showed up in my mailbox. One was on being human and the other was written by a seventy-eight-year-old woman stating what she would do differently if she had her life to live over again. I have asked all the people I know if they put the poems in my mailbox, and they all say no. What a riot. I am still laughing!

ANA RODRIGUEZ, TEXAS

One time I was trying to make a decision in my career. I felt very composed. It was a weekend, and when I woke up I went to the kitchen to make coffee. I noticed a little heart-shaped stone on the counter. I thought my son had brought it in, because we are always collecting pieces of nature that we feel have special energy. I asked him if he had found it for me, and he said no. Then I asked my life partner and got another no. Nobody else had been visiting that day.

I knew the stone was an answer from my angels telling me that they loved me and that I had made the right decision and that I must love myself and be okay with it. It is incredible that the stone is exactly in a heart shape.

I am the receptionist in my company, and every day people come to my desk to get their ANGEL® Card for the day. I can see the difference in their attitude and energy because of the angels! The news has spread over the company that "angels give you messages in the reception area." People are getting the idea that to start the day in a positive way, with positive feelings, they can come to see what the angels have to say.

PAT THOMPSON, VIRGINIA

This happened about eleven years ago. My uncle Bill had terminal cancer. He'd done fairly well with the illness until he started chemotherapy and went steadily downhill after that. Shortly before he went into the hospital for the last time, his wife, my aunt Molly, awoke early one morning to the sound of laughter and talking. She and my uncle had separate bedrooms at the time. She looked out her window and she saw "three angels walking by, talking and laughing with one another." She never told her husband about this. Then one night after he'd been taken to the hospital, my aunt was reluctant to leave for home because he was so sick. He told her to go on home and not to worry about him. That he was never alone. There were always *three* others with him.

ALLAN P. DUNCAN, NEW JERSEY

I've experienced many miracles in my life. I'm a former highly decorated police officer who for many years only experienced the darker side of life. All I saw was violence, anger, death, and despair, and it affected me deeply. I lost my faith in God on March 28, 1975. It was Good Friday, and I was involved in a gunfight with a psychopath who ended up shooting three police officers, two of whom were killed. I watched the wounded officers bleed to death since there was no way to save them. I remember being barricaded behind a tree, crying and feeling both helpless and useless. I wondered how God could allow such a thing to happen on Good Friday.

I couldn't accept reality as I experienced it, so I sought refuge in a bottle. Within several years, I was a hopeless alcoholic. I was in and out of state mental hospitals, detox, and rehabs. I ended up homeless, living in the woods. I seriously attempted suicide several times, and yet I couldn't die! I was involved in a car accident in which my car was ripped in half, and yet I lived and through all this I wondered why I couldn't die.

I've been sober ten years, thanks to the help and love of many angelic souls. They loved me when I couldn't love myself, and they nurtured me back to health. I realized that there had to be a higher power that had protected me through my dark times, and I sought that power. I realized that there had to be a reason for me living through my hell and that there must be a purpose for me being alive. It was through a support group for recovering alcoholics that I made peace with God and found my way back to the spiritual path.

Today I'm a social worker who works with emotionally disturbed children. I am also a musician, poet, and painter. I have a show in New Hope now of my paintings, and it's receiving rave reviews. One of my paintings is a portrait of the Dalai Lama. I was blessed by him in 1984, and I'm doing work with the U.S. Tibet Committee to help free his country. Holy men from India and Tibet have been coming to the show not knowing what was there, and the owner of the gallery said he has never experienced anything like this before. The holy men stated that they were drawn to the gallery and then discovered my paintings. One of them left me a gold Buddhist pendant personally blessed by the Dalai Lama before he returned to India. I am starting a series of angel paintings now!

For Christmas my friends all gave me angels, and I have them all over my bedroom. I made an altar of Buddhas and angels, and I place my angel mail beneath a large Buddha. I burn rose incense and listen to "Angel Love" by Aeoliah while I write my letters and then meditate daily before I go to work. The past several months have been magnificent since I have brought the angels into my practices.

Some of my favorite quotations are: "The difference between a stumbling block and a stepping-stone is how you use it" and "Pain is the touchstone to all spiritual growth." In my life, this has been true. I look back on my painful past as a great learning experience, and realize that I wouldn't be where I am now if I hadn't experienced my personal hell.

KATHY LYNN KLINGER, INDIANA

My angels are always apparent in my life. When I was eight-and-a-half-months pregnant and had a twenty-month-old, my husband had been laid off from work and severely depressed for eight months. We had what appeared to be no money. His unemployment had run out, and we had bills and no food. On the way home from the obstetrician, my husband kept saying we had no money and I kept telling him that God would always take care of us, that I didn't know how, but I knew that he would.

When we got home, in the mail was a bank statement showing that money had been deposited in our account. My husband was sure it was a mistake, and I didn't want to spend money that was not ours, so I called the bank. They assured me that someone had come in and asked that it be put in our account and that we should feel free to use it. So we could eat. God had blessed us.

Several months later, my husband got back to work, and we received a phone call from the bank saying that they had just found the money was put in the wrong Michael Klinger's account. They knew I had called, but the error had just been found. They were sorry and asked if we could pay back the money a little at a time. Well, now of course we could, because my husband was working. So angels can even arrange loans when no one else can!!!

DOTTI WHEELER, CALIFORNIA

I thank you for pointing out in your book that it is indeed possible for angels to come up to people in unusual places — like bars. Several years ago, when I was going through a difficult time in my life, I had just such an experience.

The angel called herself Judy, and she advised me not to share this story with people because they may "put it down" since the experience took place in a bar. I am not now, nor have I ever been, a heavy drinker. At the time of this event, I worked a 4:00 p.m. to midnight shift at a 7-11 store. I had no car, and was renting a small bedroom connected to a somewhat seedy restaurant/bar. I was having dizzy spells at the time that no one knew about. Judy did know and told me not to worry about it; she said it had something to do with the Holy Spirit. She also told me I had absolutely no idea how much God loved me and how precious I was. This part has made me cry every time I have related this story to anyone. She told me that I should stop repeating my prayers, that I had already been heard. She said I shouldn't try to "outline" how the things I wanted were going to come about. She said God wanted far more for me than I could ever think to ask for.

She also told me I would forget about my conversation with her, which was wrong — I'll never forget it. She told me I should always remember to give the credit to God and not let my ego take credit when "the changes" took place in my life. Judy also told me that there would be a time of darkness before things got better. Darkness indeed! About a year later I woke up in the hospital with my eyes bandaged after an eye operation. She encouraged me to hang on to the light at the end of the tunnel when I hit this difficult period of my life and said it was extremely difficult to translate heavenly time to earth time, and she didn't want to be pinned down as to when these changes would take place. By the way, the bar was a funky neighborhood bar, with only regular customers; very few strangers came in. She was dressed in a gray suit with a white blouse, prim and proper, looking like a schoolteacher or librarian. Very out of place in there!

It has been about seven years now. I feel I have experienced the bad part, but not the good so far. Two summers ago I spent three months living in my car —

a very bleak time in my life. I would love to read other stories of people's unusual encounters with the angels.

KATHY FAULSTICH, NEVADA

I can't remember exactly when this happened to my husband, Vern. I think it was about fifteen years ago.

For four days Vern kept getting a message several times a day while he was wide awake, at his desk, at work, or watching TV. The message was: "Look for the boy with the rose." Over and over this came to him. He always said his uncle Bud was his "private angel," so he assumed the message was coming from him.

On day four of the messages, Vern went to a coffee shop he hadn't been to in at least five years. He sat at the counter next to a young boy about sixteen or seventeen years old. The boy had a small pastry and a glass of water in front of him, and Vern remarked that someone young and strong needed more to eat than that. The boy gave him a dirty look and said, "_____ off, mister."

Vern asked him, "What's your problem, son?"

No answer came. Vern asked again, and this time the boy said, "None of your _____ business, mister."

At this point the boy reached for his glass of water with his left hand and Vern saw a tattoo of a rose on the inside of his left arm just below the elbow. Vern knew now that this was the young boy he was to find and help. He started to question the boy again about what was wrong, and finally the boy said, "What's your problem, mister?"

Vern said, "I don't have a problem, but you do, and I was sent to help you."

The boy looked at Vern and said, "What are you, mister, some kind of a nut?"

"Yes," Vern replied. "I've been called a nut, and more, lots of times, but I never let it bother me — because I'm a very special 'nut.' I can help people solve big problems in their lives, so you may as well tell me yours because I'm not going to leave here until you do!"

The boy said, "Well, no one can help me, not even a nut. My life is one giant mess, and the only way out is suicide and I have a foolproof plan. Want to hear about it, mister?"

"No," said Vern. "I just want to know *why*, not *how*."

The boy went on to explain that his parents were his one and only problem (or so he thought). His parents took away his gold earring, his stereo, his car, and his allowance, and insisted he work harder at school, go to church, read one book a month, and so on. He was also required to spend three nights a week at home! Vern tried to keep a straight face during all this explanation, but a smile creased Vern's face and the boy became even angrier! "It's not funny, mister. My life is hell. I have no freedom at all, I have a year at school to go, and I just can't take it anymore; I'll be better off dead, and then 'they' can live with it — they are killing me!"

It was then that Vern got serious and began to put a theory of his into words. "Let me tell you something way out in left field that may help you. Just listen to me for a few minutes, and then if you still feel the same way, you and I will shake hands and I'll leave, okay?"

The boy said, "Okay, but don't preach or yell the way they do twenty-four hours a day!"

Vern began to explain one of his very favorite metaphysical theories, and the boy's face turned calm and childlike. "I'm not sure why your parents have set down all these rules — the reason could be love or whatever — but that is not important here." The boy looked startled but kept quiet while Vern continued. "I think you need to realize that *you* picked these two people to be your mom and dad."

The boy interjected, "No way, mister. I would never pick out anyone that mean. By the way, how could I have picked them? I wasn't even born when they met. This is crazy; you really are nuts!"

Vern continued, "I believe in reincarnation, and I also believe that between your last life and this one, when you were at rest in the universe, your soul-spirit (the part of you that never dies) looked around for a set of earthly parents. You needed one male and one female to come together so you could have a vehicle of entry for your physical body. Your soul-spark took up residence in that body, and here you are. So stop and think of all that hatred you have for this man and woman. You looked down on earth from the universe, and you found one male and one female out of all the people on earth. You liked what you saw, you liked their values, and you started to pull strings from the other side to get these two people together so you could be part of their family in this life. Maybe the

next time around you may pick someone different, or
you may pick them again. So, I'd like you to think
about all these bad feelings you have now. Don't you
think in view of the fact it was you who picked them
out, and not the other way around, that these feelings
you have about killing yourself are way off base?"

There was a long pause, and with a certain calm
not there before the boy said, "Mister, you really
believe what you just told me, don't you?"

Vern said, "Yes, think about the possibility that
you chose to be a member of your family. Maybe your
friends at school think your parents are too old-
fashioned, or maybe you are a headstrong kid who
needs a good kick in the pants. Whatever the reason,
remember that you liked what you saw from the other
side long ago. Go home and take a good look at what
you see. Try and talk to your parents this time and listen to them. Ask them to listen to you. If you want me
to go with you, I will, but try it — don't look for a miracle right away. Living is hard work for you and your
parents, but give them a chance. Work it out, work
hard. You can do it. Then, if you feel that it is too tough
to live at home, leave when you are eighteen. Join the
Navy, go to school, live your own life. Remember, you
wanted this life, so live it — don't *end* it!"

With tears in his eyes, the boy said, "Mister, you
are still nuts, but what you said is so far-out it must be
partly true. At least you care. Thanks, man."

He left the coffee shop, and Vern never saw him
again. But I did, on the day I buried Vern. A tall
young man in his early thirties came up to me and

said, "I had to come today. I wanted to say good-bye and thanks to Vern. He helped me out once, and now I have a beautiful wife and two kids. I still don't get along with my parents very well, but we talk and visit once in a while."

I asked, "Who are you?"

He said, "The boy with the rose" and held out his arm for me to see.

KATIE, AIT (ANGEL IN TRAINING)

We were on a trip across the country, on our way back to Oregon. We had been driving all day and finally stopped at a motel out of sheer sleepiness. It was not the nicest place, but it was late at night and the choices were few. I was to sleep in a folding bed in the living room. As I unfolded the bed, I noticed that inside the bed was a card — like a Christmas gift card — with an angel on it and on the back it said: "To: Katie, From: Grandma." I was amazed and very happy. I still carry the card with me today as a gentle angel reminder that the angels are always with us no matter where we go.

Children and Angels

I have always known I had a guardian angel looking out for me. I don't remember when I was first told about my guardian angel, or if it was even a human being who told me. My earliest guardian angel memories are of feelings — wonderful feelings of grace, magic, beauty, and a oneness with all the life vibrating in my extra-large backyard. Memories of floating to sleep with a golden light that let me know I was never alone. My experience of angels has always been more than just a belief; it is a knowing deep inside me that began long before I entered the earth realm. I was born knowing I had an angel with me. You may think, Well, sure, that is easy to say — we can all invent our past however we like. My confirmation of this knowing comes now through experiences of children in my life and stories their parents have told me. Many parents are finding out that their children believe in angels, even when they have never mentioned the idea to them and have no reason to think any other adult has.

I have two nieces and a nephew who taught me quite a lot about angels when they were little kids, as well as about joy and hilarity. When I was writing my first book about angels, I asked my nieces to tell me some things about angels. Their answers were great! Jessica, who was four at the time, told me that angels probably glow in the dark and then stated in a confident way, "Of course, we know they have feet." We all laughed hysterically at this statement. Then something very special happened. Elizabeth, who was eight at the time, wrote a poem about angels for my first book and began to read it (the same poem that opened this chapter). When she came to the line that said, "And I know you can't put your hand out and touch them," Jessica, who was listening very attentively, got a strange look on her face and reached her arm out behind her and moved it around as if she were trying to reach for something in the dark. I had two thoughts: One, she assumes that her angel is standing right behind her all the time, and, two, it has never occurred to her that she won't be able to feel her angel with her hand.

I have found that most children who are aware of angels naturally think of angels as protection, and also that children have their own little worries and fears, and angels help them relieve these fears and worries. If we can teach children about angels in an open, nonfearful, and accepting way, perhaps the patterns of fear and worry that humans seem to incur simply by being on the earth will not be such a problem in their later years. If you are already aware that your children know about angels or if you have told them about angels, reassure them every day that their angels love and protect them. Children are so creative that they will expand their relationship with angels in their own ways. If allowed and encouraged in a positive and simple way, children's relationship with their angels will be a gift for their parents. Children and angels never fail to bring me joy and laughter. Sometimes, just being in the presence of a child or an infant is a true angel experience. Children's angel experiences are of such a pure nature that they provide direct confirmation that angels exist. I bet many parents are finding this out today. The following letters, which first appeared in *Answers from the Angels*, are from parents talking about their children and their children's experiences with angels.

CHRISTINA L. ROSS, NORTH CAROLINA

As I was reading the first pages of *Messengers of Light*, a wonderful synchronism occurred, which I would like to share with you.

I have twin daughters, named Katie and Amy, who are truly blessings from God. They are ten years old, and without having knowledge of my reading your book, they came to me with a beautiful tale of angel help. Many months went by before they told me their story because they were afraid they would "get in trouble" for being careless. I will relate the experience in the words of Amy as she saw it — her imagery was so enchanting!

AMY: "We were swinging on the swing set out in the backyard and had put our pet rabbits down on the ground to play. As Katie began to swing, her rabbit Priscilla hopped under the swing set where Katie's feet would have touched the ground. Katie said that if she kept swinging high enough, her feet wouldn't kick the rabbit. She was swinging so high she went way above the edge of the garage roof [twelve feet high]. Then Katie's foot got caught on the swing bar [support post] and pulled her out of the swing way up in the air. Then I saw something so magical I couldn't believe it. Katie turned a complete flip [360 degrees] in slow motion and landed on her bottom in the grass, barely missing Priscilla! On each side of her was one boy angel and one girl angel and lots of pretty colors like dark pink and light pink and pale blue and yellow, but I could still see Katie and her clothes through the colors! Where the angels were touching her, on her shoulders and hips, was a real pretty white light, and she landed so softly for being so high up in the air. I'll never forget what I saw!"

Well, as you can guess, I was sitting there with my mouth open. Then I had an uncontrollable desire to burst out laughing! Which I did. The girls were so shocked that they weren't in trouble for swinging so high or for putting their rabbit's life in peril that they had tears in their eyes. I told Katie to thank the angels for their help and to consider what might have happened had they not helped her in her carelessness. She explained that even though she couldn't feel them touching her, she knew in her heart everything was going to be okay even though she was falling.

Coincidentally (ha ha), my mother, whom I hadn't talked to for over two months, called the same day and I related this story to her over the phone. After I finished telling her what her granddaughter Amy had seen, she said, "This is unbelievable! A friend of mine has just left my house and we have spent the last six hours or so talking about that very subject — angels! I've never given them much thought until now, but you better believe I will in the future."

I said, "Mom, the longer I live, the more I realize that things happen for a reason. And ours is not to question, but to be thankful for each and every episode the angels bring to us."

I love the way Christina let her children know that it is a good idea to show the angels gratitude for their help and to use the experience as a positive lesson in life.

DON KERR, WASHINGTON

What I want to write about is my son Gavin. He is a multiple-handicapped child with Down's syndrome, Klinefelter's syndrome, and epilepsy who is partially disabled. He seemingly has three or four strikes against him, but I believe he is of the angelic realm. His whole personality just shines with humor, cheerfulness, and love. He never lets my wife and me get into an argument. He steps in and puts an end to our little row. He is at present going to summer day camp for the handicapped, and the counselors up there all fight to get him in their group. They all love him because he is so cheerful and cooperative.

Do you think I have an angel in the house? When I take him to church, the pastor tells me he voluntarily greets people as they come into church. The pastor told me he has given the members of the church a great lesson in love. Isn't that what angels do best?

JOSHUA G. AND MARY G., COLORADO AND GEORGIA

Letter 1

I don't know if I should be writing and telling you this. My son Joshua, who is six, has an angel he talks to all the time. Joshua met her at the babysitter's house. Joshua says her name is Brenda. He told me he is the only one who can see her; she won't let me see her. She goes everywhere with Joshua. Brenda was telling Joshua how his dad was doing when he was in Saudi Arabia during the war. It was so exciting. I knew my husband would be okay! Joshua says Brenda stays in his room now; she was always going to the mountains where she lives. Joshua says Brenda and her family were killed in the mountains. He told me how he talks to Brenda. In his words: "Her mind talks to my mind, and my mind talks to hers. We don't talk the way you and I do."

Letter 2

Everything is going really well for us. Our lives have changed a lot — I would have to say because of

Joshua. We had to move to Georgia; my husband got restationed. I was going to send Joshua and his younger brother by plane, and I was going to drive out with my oldest son and three cats. It turned out that we all drove together, but when Joshua thought he was going to fly, he said that Brenda would keep him and his younger brother, Brandon, safe, and that I wouldn't need her because her dad was going to be with me.

I said, "Who's that?"

Joshua replied, "You know, God."

I said, "Fine, I can definitely handle that."

The drive from Colorado to Georgia was great, and Brenda watched out for the whole family on the way. The last thing that has to be said is that Brenda wants Joshua to pray a lot, and she prays with him. She has also taken him to a lot of castles. He drew a picture of one, and it looked pretty good. He said almost every night Brenda takes him somewhere.

Angel Journaling

One day on the Internet, I found Lila*Star's angel-guide website and loved it (the site address is included in the Resources section at the back of this book). This website provides a great example of bringing the angels into our everyday life, with love, light, and grace. In her "Angel Gatherings" section ("A Diary of Angel Encounters, Songs, Art, Media, Visions, Emotions") — a great example of angel journaling — I delighted in the following wonderful entry and contacted her for permission to share it with you in this book.

LILA*STAR

My daughter (four) and I were lying in bed this morning, greeting our toes with a good morning tickle and waking up snuggling together. We welcomed the angels as we have been doing every morning for a while now, and thanked them for a restful night. We do a little mini-meditation whereby we send some healing light to those who need it. Today we sent some to my father who could do with some healing for his poor intestine, and we sent some to Babe's cousin Jo, who just had her appendix out.

Then I said, "Let's ask the angels to send some healing light to Dad in his office..."

"NOOO," she said. I asked why not, to which she replied, "He is not ill, he does not need healing." Fair enough I thought, but I also saw her thinking. A few minutes later she said, "Do you know what?"

"What?" I said.

She replied, "There are really two kinds of angel light, the Healing Light and the Make Happy Light" ...and it made me smile — and right she is, from today we are also dispensing Make Happy Light to those who could use a little cheering up.

Children of the Sun

When you combine art, music, story, and divine light, the result is angelic. My friend Laurel Savoie was *called* to produce a very special project for children of all ages. *Children of the Sun* is a high-quality, full-color picture book with an enlightening story, combined with beautiful songs and background music on a companion CD to enhance the experience. I can't say enough about *Children of the Sun*; it *is* an angel experience — a perfectly wonderful tool for expanding your angel consciousness and reminding yourself of the sweet, innocent, funny, and truly special little child within you. Your inner child says to look in the Resources section at the back of this book to find out how to visit Laurel's website and get a copy of this magical book with CD!

LAUREL SAVOIE, LOUISIANA

When Terry Lynn asked me to write something about my book, I was honored. Yet, for a while I struggled with the question "Where do I start?" How does one go about describing a life-altering experience? How do you put into words the deep knowing and personal fulfillment that comes from creating something that represents the sum total of your life's work, both in spirit and in the arts?

The journey began in 1995. While interacting with a very special child (the child within me), I began writing songs that communicated deep spiritual truths in a very fun and childlike way. These songs, combined with the pure intention of creating a useful teaching tool for parents, relatives, and teachers of the new children, became *Children of the Sun: A Spiritual Journey for Children of All Ages*. From humble beginnings, through the power of intention and perfection, came a multimedia book created especially to stimulate the spiritual growth process in the children of the new earth. During the six years that it took to complete the project, the process was charged with the intent of perfection from its very inception until June 2001, when the entire production and printing process was completed and we had the book and CD in hand — all the while realizing that perfection cannot be rushed or forced. When our intention is pure and we accept and allow things to unfold naturally, without resistance and interference, everything can bloom into a beautiful flower — if we can only allow ourselves to just "let go and let God."

As a seeker of truth, my early years were lived with a deeply felt desire to know who I am and why I am here. I needed to know "the truth, the whole truth and nothing but the truth" of my being. Until the underlying spiritual principles of life were revealed to me, I could not rest. Those many years of seeking out the truth taught me that with intent and earnest determination, the perfection of my life and the lives of others around me would be revealed. In the perfection of seeking, answers would come and provide the meaning, clarity, and illumination that I needed at that moment to go on in what appeared to be a mysteriously dark and unjust world.

During the making of *Children of the Sun*, many of our friends and peers brought to the table their unique talents, abilities, and creativity to help make my vision a reality. Terry Lynn is one of the friends who was instrumental in this process. I know how blessed I am to be friends with "TLT." When we met, it was love at first sight. Terry is such a bright light and literally an angel as a friend and so easy to love. When it came time to assign a voice to each of the eleven characters in *Children of the Sun*, Terry Lynn was the obvious choice to play "the Angel." From the moment she agreed to do it, the perfect experience began to unfold as if by magic.

My husband, Larry, and I live in New Orleans, and Terry Lynn lives in Southern California, where we used to live. So, Larry booked studio time there, and we orchestrated a plan to drive to Los Angeles to record the Angel (Terry Lynn) and another mutual friend, Abigail Lewis, to play "the Voice." After that, Larry and I would drive on to Tucson, Arizona, to record our friend Bruce Silvey as the voice of Moses. We were really looking forward to these recording sessions and having fun with our friends again. The plan and timing seemed perfect. However, when I telephoned Terry with our schedule, it turned out that she was going to be in Sedona at that time, working with her friend Peter Sterling, the wonderful harpist she had spoken so highly of.

The eleven songs I wrote for the story had already been recorded. However, we still needed the perfect background music and harp to fill in at the appropriate times throughout the story. Terry suggested that we record her voice in Peter's recording studio. Just for a second I thought, Oh no, it's all been planned for Los Angeles. Then I remembered perfection and I knew the angels had a better plan for us. So we extended our trip to include Sedona, a beautiful and powerful vortex area, which we had visited many times, and off we went to one of our favorite enchanted places. While in Sedona we recorded Terry's angelic voice and then heard the beautiful music from Peter's new CD with Terry singing on it. We knew that this would be the perfect heavenly background music we needed. Then, Peter played his harp live and we recorded it for the additional celestial sounds. So, being in Sedona brought the added sound of Peter's music and Terry's beautiful "angelic ahs" resounding throughout the story of the twin Dolphins of Light taking Jeremy, age seven, and his sister, Heather, age eleven, on a magical journey over the rainbow and into the Light. It was the perfect union. We were absolutely delighted.

Many of the children embodying now are being called Indigo and Crystal Children, and know only LOVE. They are advanced Light Beings, who are born with an entirely different keynote (each of us has a keynote). They function poorly in low vibrational frequencies. They are not motivated by fear but by LOVE, and from the feedback we have received from some of their mothers and other family members, they respond very well to *Children of the Sun*.

Remaining true to the idea of exposing children of all ages to spiritual truths and principles through the art of storytelling, the magic of music and sacred sounds, and beautiful visual art has brought many blessings of perfection into my life. I am looking forward to living in a world that these children will cocreate and to a time when we all realize that "We Are All One," and unite our energies with one another, the angels, and the elementals. Through this union, we can and will cocreate a new world filled with love, harmony, and peace, perfectly.

Harp Magic

I met Peter Sterling, acclaimed harpist and artist, when we were both living in Ojai, California. We became fast friends and have had many wonderful adventures together. One of my favorite times was when he came with me to Juvenile Hall in Los Angeles when I was facilitating a creative writing class, and brought his harp to play for my writers. The following week when I went back alone, one of the writers said, "Where is Peter? I need to hear some harp music so I can de-stress." The rest of the writers all expressed something similar. I hope you have the chance to hear Peter play his harp in person; if not, get one of his CDs, relax, light a candle, and let the angels take you on an exquisite journey of love. You can find out how to contact Peter by referring to the Resources section at the back of this book.

PETER STERLING, ARIZONA

Around the time of my twenty-eighth birthday, I made the decision to devote myself full-time to the pursuit of artistic excellence in stained glass. The visions that had been revealed to me were too compelling, and I knew from a place deep inside that I was to find a way to express the beauty and power I had experienced in a form that others might enjoy as well. Through a synchronistic turn of events, I found myself guided to move to the New Age mecca of Sedona, Arizona — a move that would change the course of my life forever.

The towering red-rock formations and ancient canyons called to me with an uncanny feeling of home.

I found myself drawn into the back country, where I would hike by myself for hours into the ancient canyons of the Anasazi. Oftentimes I would climb to the top of a red-rock ridge overlooking a grand vista and play my native flute, honoring the spirits of the ancestors who lived there hundreds of years before. The sound of my flute would float on the air and reverberate off the canyon walls, creating the effect of playing in a great cathedral.

As I would walk the sandy trails in silent contemplation, I would hear in the silence the voices of the ancient ones speaking to me in my heart and soul. Words of wisdom and sacred teachings would be given to me as I would humbly request that the elders share their story with me. Oftentimes vivid pictures would come into my mind as I was shown what it must have been like to live there thousands of years ago.

Meditation became effortless as I would hike back into the silent canyons and find a special place to sit and journey within. I noticed that the quieter I became, the more a golden light began to appear in my mind's eye. Radiant and warm like honey, this light enveloped me in a cocoon of peace and love like nothing I had ever experienced.

Allowing myself to move even deeper into the silence, I began to hear subtle impressions of what seemed to me to be music of some kind. Faint at first, the more I "tuned in" to it, the louder it became, until I was able to perceive this divine symphony in all its glory. The sound was like nothing I have ever heard before. It was symphonic and orchestral in nature but grander than anything I had heard previously. It had the most beautiful melody, richly layered in harmony, that rolled on and on and on. An unchained melody playing endlessly into eternity brought uncontrollable tears to my eyes — tears of joy that washed my soul of lifetimes of grief, sorrow, and sadness.

At first I was startled by what I was hearing. I opened my eyes several times and looked around, trying to figure out where this music was coming from. It seemed to me to be emanating out from everything around me — not only on the inside but also coming from the trees and the rocks and the birds and the wind. In many books I had read accounts of "the music of the spheres." Many mystics have spoken of a heavenly music that is perceived by spiritual aspirants as they move into higher states of awareness. As this was happening to me, I was keenly aware that I was experiencing some sort of spiritual initiation. I felt the presence of my spiritual guides with me, encouraging me to let go and journey deeper into this experience.

As I sat in meditation, immersed in this glorious music, I heard an inner voice that spoke to me and told me that it was safe to let go and travel on this musical sound current. I was familiar with the concept of astral travel or "out-of-body experiences" from reading different books on the subject over the years. And now as I sat there on a rock in the canyon, it was as though the heavens were opening up to me and I was being invited in to this magical realm.

As I did this, my inner vision opened up simultaneously, and I was able to perceive, to my astonishment, angels floating right before my eyes. I couldn't believe what I was seeing. I tried to clear my mind of any self-created images, but they just stayed there in front of me, looking at me and smiling. As their image became clearer I was able to perceive that they were cherubs. Cherubs are the little, chubby-baby-type angels that we see so often depicted in Renaissance art. They were playing instruments like harps, violins, and flutes, and the music they were playing was the same music that I was hearing before I saw them. There was a whole flock of them, and they flew around me with great excitement as they beckoned me to come with them on a journey into their world.

Soaring and flying through iridescent, prismatic colors, I followed my angel guides as they lead me on a journey into the angelic realms. The feeling was one of pure joy and exhilaration as together we flew through one realm of indescribable beauty after another. If you have ever gazed into a beautiful quartz crystal with a colored light illuminating it and let your imagination explore the interior of it, you might get an idea of what this was like for me. Eventually we came to a place where all I saw up ahead of me was a luminous sphere of radiant light that shone like a thousand suns. The light was so bright that I had a hard time looking at it. The energy coming from it was one of pure love, which penetrated me deeply into the very core of my heart and soul. I was drawn to it like a moth to a flame, but my angel guides held me back, for it wasn't time for me to merge totally with this luminous sphere of flaming love.

As I continued to gaze upon it with squinting eyes, I began to see that radiating out in all directions from it were more angels of every shape and size imaginable. There were multitudes of them, and they were all singing in perfect harmony praises to this Light, the Source of All Things. This was the source of the music that I was hearing and that my angel guides were playing. They told me that in reality there is only one song. The one song expresses all the love, harmony, peace, and oneness that emanate directly from God out into the far reaches of every corner of the universe.

This is the "song of creation." I was told that once upon a time all the beings on earth heard this song and sang it with one another in perfect harmony. This was back in the time of the Garden of Eden, before the fall. But in the present time most beings of earth don't hear this celestial music anymore. The result of this is apparent everywhere we look, as the people of earth feel disconnected from the Source of All Things. The angels told me that the volume is being turned up on God's heavenly music, so that once again the people of earth can hear this divine symphony and come back into a state of peace, love, and harmony. It is a "clarion call" to the souls of earth to come home once again into the Love. The term they used to describe it to me was *ascension*. The love and light are increasing everywhere as God calls all his children home.

As this grand vision was shared with me, it was revealed that my sacred mission was to help bring this heavenly music to earth once again. They told me that with their help I would begin to play music and become a channel for the celestial symphony. And to top it all off, they showed me that the instrument that I would play would be the harp.

At first I was resistant to this heavenly request. How could I be a musician bringing forth the heavenly music when I myself had very little musical experience and no training whatsoever? But they assured me that if I was willing to embark on this journey with them, they would take care of everything. Like many people, I had felt music in my heart for many years, and now it was time to bring it out.

Almost immediately, synchronistic events started to happen. Within a few days of having this vision, I met a woman in town who was a harpist. I told her my curiosity about the harp, and she told me that she happened to have a small harp for sale and if I'd like I could come by her place to try it. From the first moment I put my hands on the harp, I knew this was what I was looking for. I purchased the harp and began playing it several hours a day. Music seemed to come out of it effortlessly as my fingers would move on the strings almost by themselves. The harp had a small carrying case, and I loved to carry it back into the canyons to find a special place to sit and play for the rocks, the birds, and the wind.

As I would strum the harp, I could hear the angels' voices lofting in the overtones and singing with me as I would play. I devoted myself wholeheartedly to the task at hand and immersed myself into the world of the harp. Every chance I had I would sit and play, as distinct melodies and songs began to take form within a matter of weeks. There was a distinct energy that would come over me when I would play. I could literally put my hands to the strings and relax and watch as my fingers would move on the strings by themselves.

At first I was a little frightened by what was occurring, but I continued to hear the gentle encouragement of the angels to surrender and allow this music to come through me. Oftentimes my eyes would start to tear uncontrollably when I would play, and I would sweat profusely as the energy would come through. Some years later I realized that I had a special angel harp teacher who would merge with my energy field and play through me, teaching me by allowing me to feel what it was like to play. It was happening very fast and at times I couldn't believe what was unfolding, so I would sit in front of a mirror and play so I could see for myself that it was true.

After a series of life events and travels, I was shown that I would record a professional recording and that this music was going to go out all over the world. I even saw an image of a finished CD in a catalogue with other music. At my first session in the studio, I prayed to the angels to play through me. For an hour and a half I sat at the harp as the music came through and tears flowed from my eyes. This first session gave me the harp tracks that the rest of the music was built upon. Magical happenings and synchronicities were happening on a daily basis as this special music was being created. When it was all done I asked the angels what we should call it, and the response I heard was *Harp Magic* — of course, as this is what my whole experience has been with the harp.

I made fifty copies of the CD and began giving them out to friends and strangers alike, and the response was an overwhelming affirmation of the angels' wish. People loved the music, and a couple of New Age bookstores even offered to sell it for me. Wow! I thought to myself. This is exactly the way the angels told me it would be. Now I found myself having to promote and market this special music from the angels, but I knew nothing of the "business of music." So once again I called on my trusty angel guides to help. I told them if they wanted this music to go out to the world, would they please send me some help with this part of it.

Within a week of asking for assistance, I received a phone call. On the other end was a record company executive who was traveling through Sedona on holiday. He told me he had happened to walk into one of the New Age bookstores where they were playing my music on the sound system in the store. He said he was struck by the beauty of the music and inquired about it to the store clerk. I was offered a record contract for five more albums and worldwide distribution. I fell off my chair screaming, crying, and laughing all at the same time. I couldn't believe how swiftly the angels had answered my prayer to send help!

In the fall of 1994 *Harp Magic* was released internationally to critical acclaim. It has been ten years now since the initial release of *Harp Magic*, and I have

received hundreds of letters from people all over the
world who have shared their stories of healing miracles, beautiful visions, and angelic visitations from
listening to the music. Connecting and working with
the angels brought a new ray of light into my life,
which has been a constant source of inspiration, wonder, and joy. I am constantly amazed at the synchronicity and miracle magic that the angels work in the lives
of many people I know all over the world. In these
troubled and uncertain times, I am relieved to know
that the angels are watching over us with unwavering
vigilance and steadfast companionship, guiding us all
to our souls' glorious destiny in the Light.

The Divine Artistry of Arthur Douët

Following is an interview I did with the artist Arthur Douët for
the magazine *Angel Times*. When Arthur enters a room, it
seems that everyone's heart lightens at his presence. I remember the first moment I met him; it was at the Calling All Angels
conference in Lake Whitney, Texas, in October 1994. Before
we were introduced, I felt a smile forming deep in my soul, and
I knew that I was in the presence of someone whose heart is
open and loving. Most people call him Douët, but I can't help
calling him by his first name, Arthur, because his kindness and
gentle ways remind me of King Arthur. Arthur did not "just
arrive on the scene." He has been painting angels (in this lifetime) since 1976, and he has a very grounded spiritual and art
background. He is a wise and humble man, and his art is his
way of physically transmitting love and divine inspiration to

the world (you can find out how to contact him in the Resources section at the back of this book).

TERRY LYNN TAYLOR: Did you have a moment of tran-
scendence or spiritual awareness that set you out
on the path of the divine truth you share with us in
your art?

ARTHUR DOUËT: In Paris, while studying at l'École des
Beaux Arts, I had a spiritual awakening. I went up
to the rooftop at night to meditate. I was gazing
into the stars and listening; in the state of listening
I felt the All and the beauty of the Oneness of
the universe. I felt enraptured with the intensity
and vastness of the cosmos. When I came back and
went to bed around midnight, I was awakened at
about two or three o'clock in the morning to feel
an energy flow through me from the crown of
the head downward into the spine. It was such a
wonderful feeling, and yet it was so strong it was
almost scary because I couldn't move a finger and
I didn't understand what was going on with me.
This began happening each night, and I was very
thankful that it didn't happen during the day in the
streets of Paris. And then I learned to release
the fear by saying to the Infinite One, "Into your
hands I commit my spirit." The energy flow and
feeling of expansion was so great that it showed
me that something was really going on as a result
of meditating, which someone explained later to
me as my light body superimposing over the
physical.

TERRY: It sounds to me like you were seized by the Holy Spirit.

ARTHUR: Yes, I guess you could call it that. I wanted to give my life and my art to communicate the light I was receiving in my being. When I moved to Houston in 1976, I had a dream where I saw an angel walking across a room with a high ceiling, defying gravity, coming toward me at an angle. He/she had a winglike structure and was more real than real life, more detailed than anything I could remember. I called it a dream, but perhaps I was there experiencing it on a different level. Right after that vision I saw another vision like a painting of the Christ healing the man born blind. It didn't stay for long, but I knew that dream was outlining my mission to paint the angels, and to create through the paintings the force of light as the real reason for being. This idea of light, the Light, is not really electrical light. However, when Christ was transfigured, there was a shining light that was seen, and it very much seems to be like electrical light. So in that particular instance, the transfiguration had the same effect of light that you would see with the angels. Christ raised his vibration to the point where his disciples saw him as shining light, and it was so bright they could hardly look at it. The Light spoken of in holy writ is really the awareness of the God presence, but I think that there is also an electrical effect. It fascinates me, the use of the word *light*, such as *inner light*. My prerogative in painting has been to show a sense of inner light.

TERRY: After having your vision, you began painting angels. Did it happen overnight, or did an experience inspire you?

ARTHUR: I met a lady soon after the vision who clairvoyantly saw my personal angel, and I did a painting of that angel from what she told me. The name of the angel is Sonodon, which translates as "sweet sound of the One." In the center of her being is a crystal as the symbol of uninterrupted focus — one-pointedness of mind — without distraction. I got the feeling that she was an angel of enlightenment. Years after, when I published a photograph of the painting, I would meet people at different times who had an emotional experience recognizing her, and one woman came to tears, and said, "I know her so well; it is great to see her." So that started me on doing angels in my paintings.

TERRY: What sense do you experience of the angels around you when you paint?

ARTHUR: I call them angels of inspiration, and I really do not tune into any specifics in terms of names and designations, but I know the angels are there. I feel that the angels are beings of light who are designated by the Creator to work through many realms and protect their charges. The angels help transform unbalanced mental and emotional energies, but only humans can change thinking, feeling, and thought forms at will. I feel that the angels are invisible coworkers we can have a beneficial intimate relationship with. I see angels as inwardly moving light or energy waves, floating with beautiful, transparent colors. I feel angels exist as a definite reality, in a realm that parallels our own. It is like a ceiling fan that when it is turned on low you can just see the blades going around, and when you turn it on a faster speed you don't see it at all; the angels vibrate at a faster rate than we do — that is why we don't see them. Just like you, Terry; you honor your imagination, because that is the receiving faculty.

TERRY: I really feel that the imagination is a place of honesty.... Let's talk about how you begin a painting. Many of my artist friends have a ritual or a humbling process they go through before they begin a painting. What do you do?

ARTHUR: First I relax physically, close my eyes and become still in front of the canvas, and then I focus my mind inward. I imagine that my mind and spirit are hollow, becoming receptive to an inward flow of spiritual impulses. I sit in quiet meditation for a while, and then I see a shaft of light cascading through the crown of my head. It flows through my spine into the earth under my feet. To me this is truly a religious experience. I feel the light lifting me into a dimension of pure being — a place of ecstasy and vastness beyond description. With my eyes still closed, I breathe deeply three times onto the canvas and I ask the Holy Spirit to breathe through me and bless the atmosphere around the creation to come. This is my way of saying to the analytical mind, "Take a back seat and allow something divine to come through." One time when I was trying with great effort to follow the rules of a particular meditation technique, I heard a voice within say, "Why don't you just relax and let me *be* God? I am meditating through you all the time. Just listen!" At some point, an image will flow into my mind's eye, and with it comes an impulse that I know comes from the soul level. When I meditate, I get the image of the angel who needs to be done. I start to draw with my eyes closed, using my nondominant hand; at a certain point I open my eyes to see what has come through. With my eyes open, I continue to work intuitively, pulling the composition together with line and color notes.

TERRY: What exactly do you mean by color notes?

ARTHUR: The deep breathing I do draws the breath through the crown chakra all the way into the heart out to what I am painting on, and that actual transference of energy creates a force field around the painting so that the painting is like a living energy; it is like "music crystallized." Artwork vibrates; every brush stroke registers a vibration, which eventually radiates from the painting's surface and reflects the intent and consciousness of the painter. The music of the painting is waiting to be replayed to the beholder as a subliminal language, a language of the heart or feeling nature — it bypasses the intellect. Sometimes I'll hum a sound that connects me with the great creative feminine energy residing in the earth.

TERRY: You mention your love of silence and say that if you had to be identified by any particular line of religious thinking, you would be most like a Sufi and a Quaker.

ARTHUR: I love the way the Sufis talk about the Oneness, and the All One, and I love the deep silence that the Quakers practice. Legend has it that when the Native Americans came to destroy the white settlements in a certain area, they approached a Quaker settlement and saw that everyone was in a meeting hall sitting in total silence. The chief looked in and came back saying that these people worship the Great White Spirit, so they left without harming them. I have always felt that out of the silence is born music and great art, and other great innovative ideas come from the silence. I always orient myself within the silence before going into any kind of artistic expression.

An Interview with Carlos Santana

The interview with Carlos Santana included here is from the book I wrote on creativity, *Creating with the Angels*. Rereading the interview now confirms all the qualities I feel the angels are urging us to cultivate, and which Carlos himself so well embodies. I went to one of the concerts he did at the Hollywood Bowl, which is a special outdoor venue. When he came out onstage, Carlos asked the crowd to be silent and know that there were angels all around them; then he added some other wise words. The audience was made up of all ages, all races, all walks of life, and all of us were raised up by the light he shared. You could feel the positive energy permeating the crowd and beyond. The concert was a confirmation of all that Carlos Santana stands for; it is so refreshing that he is never afraid to speak of his spirituality in public appearances and interviews.

TERRY LYNN TAYLOR: First of all, I want to thank you for all your support of my book and of the angels. *Creating with the Angels* is about creativity and how the angels inspire us to be creative. So I am asking people who are leading creative lives to share how the angels inspire them.

CARLOS SANTANA: Last year, when I was reading your book, I began to notice what you call angel synchronisms, funny coincidences. I was hanging out with a friend, and I asked her if she believed in angels. She got really quiet and said, "Well, I believe that there is a Supreme Power." And I said that that Supreme Power holds a chandelier, and in the light are Jesus, Krishna, and Buddha, but the crystals are the angels.

TERRY: Oh, I love that.

CARLOS: And she said, "Oh, okay." I wanted her to know that, because I could tell by her eyes that she is a very special person. I wanted to give her something. As Paramahansa Yogananda said, "Give us thoughts and ideas to chew all day like gum — words and thoughts that our minds can chew."

TERRY: I feel like there is a lot of hope now on the planet. Do you, or do you think that things are getting really bad?

CARLOS: Oh no, no, I really feel that things are bad for people who believe that without them the world cannot go on. For them, the world is ending. I think that for people who wake up in the morning and can hardly wait to do something for someone else — for them the world is just beginning. For those of us who want to complement life and serve, our world is just beginning.

TERRY: That is an interesting way to look at it. On some level, that has to do with creativity, too, because if we feel creative, we have something to give, and helping others also gives us a reason to keep going. I know my own creativity seems to help when I get into a low point. I get the realization that I have got to do something creative, no matter what. What do you think creativity is? Do you think everyone is creative?

CARLOS: I think that creativity comes from rousing enough enthusiasm. There is nothing more contagious. When you are enthusiastic, you can go on without food; you just go on, and people want to be around you. I also think that creativity comes from having made some kind of effort to listen to your inner voice. If you listen to your inner voice, I think that you awaken enthusiasm and imagination, which is vision. And I think that these are the two wings that we need to fly.

TERRY: That's beautiful.

CARLOS: Enthusiasm and imagination.

TERRY: Do you know that *enthusiasm* means "filled with God"?

CARLOS: Really? Wow. When I was reading your book, I was sick with an ear infection. I was really dizzy. I was wondering what was wrong with me. I had serious jet lag when I was in Germany and couldn't sleep. So I started reading your book, and I was reading about what it means to be healed, and about the dictionary definition that *to heal* means "to be whole and sound." So I said, "Whole and sound." Reading your book gave me more inner strength and inner peace — the message "You're going to be all right." Then when I found out that I had an ear infection, I was relieved to know what was causing the dizziness.

TERRY: So basically that universal message came through that the angels are always trying to give us — that you are going to be okay and that the angels are looking out after you.

CARLOS: Yes. They work faster than X-rays, and they can tell you immediately: "It's okay. You are all right."

TERRY: Are the angels active in your life right now?

CARLOS: Yeah. They add to my understanding that we are all supremely important to God, yet at the same time there are some people who belong in the category of a fuse. For example, in your house you have a fuse box. All of the lights are important in every room, but if the fuse goes, the whole house goes. So I sometimes see myself as a fuse.

TERRY: So, you've created this momentum, and you have to stay with it because you are lighting up other lives.

CARLOS: Right, so I am just acknowledging that that is so, and by acknowledging this I take the responsibility of thinking more with my heart than with my mind. I make it a point to say to myself, "No, think higher, from your heart." In the last two years, it has been easier for me to think, and feel, and act, and rationalize with my heart. I find myself saying, "I'm sorry" less often because I don't step on people's toes. I don't have to shout to get a point across, and I want to let others make their point. I think that people are more won over this way than when I beat them over the head with my two cents.

TERRY: So you are communicating in a much higher way.

CARLOS: In a much clearer way, so that people can either take it or leave it.

TERRY: Does your fame get in the way of communication?

CARLOS: My mom and dad are very strong in how they raised me, but I realize that 99 percent is God's grace and the other 1 percent is personal effort. It is stupid to say, "I did it my way" like the song. Can you imagine dying and going to heaven and singing that song? The angels would leave you belly up.

TERRY: That is a very funny thought. So do you feel that your family is your stronghold?

CARLOS: Yes, because they pray for me. I know my mom prays for me, and to tell you the truth, when I play a solo on my guitar and I am onstage, I close my eyes and I feel like I am a baby in the womb. When my mom prays for me, it is direct milk for me. So that keeps me stable, and I also know that people are flowers, music is the water, and I am the hose. So that I don't have to have the headache to make it happen.

TERRY: You are just willing to do it.

CARLOS: I'm just willing to get out of the way and say, "Lord, if you want me to touch all those people, I will touch all those people." It's God's headache. I know that every time I go to Paris, the audience totally goes bananas — it's like a spiritual experience for two hours, and you can just feel it. Black and white, young and old. And it just makes me realize that the music is what liberates people from within — the tone. It makes us realize that we are worth more than the sum of it all, and I think that real music happens when someone says, "I went to that concert, and it changed my life; those three notes — when you hit those notes my hair stood up and I cried and I laughed."

TERRY: There has to be something to that. With music, I think hearts can really be touched and that the language of the heart happens. Can you tell when you are reaching hearts?

CARLOS: Oh yeah!

TERRY: It must feel really powerful.

CARLOS: Actually, it sometimes feels like you are walking uphill. Once I touch the band, and I know that if I put my hand out in front and my five fingers become one, that is how it is. You get people so alive. I can tell it's happened when even the police are dancing — they forget that they are in authority. You get someone who has to be in authority dancing and — that's when I know that the spirit is overwhelming — it has taken everybody. That is what we try to do, whether it is in Germany or Japan.

TERRY: You don't try; you do it. It happens!

CARLOS: I have been doing this, by the grace of God, since 1959, but when I played at San Quentin, I became more confident of the sound. And in Jerusalem, when the Hebrew and Palestinian people danced together at the Sultan Garden. At San Quentin, all the prisoners — Mexicans, black people, and white people — they all stayed. They told me that when B. B. King played there, all the whites and Hispanics left; only the black people stayed. But the warden said, "I don't know what it is about you, but they all stayed." At first they all had their arms crossed, like, "Okay, *do* something for me. What are you going to do?" Then their arms went down, and they started elbowing each other. Pretty soon, they were like kids in a sandbox. So that gave me, obviously, a lot of confidence.

TERRY: So you knew then that there was something more to your music than just technique — it was reaching inside of people. That is true about your music, and you do reach across the cultures.

CARLOS: That is the thing that I am waking up to, and I
think a lot of people may have trouble with it, but
I think most people will accept it. I believe that it
is really prehistoric to think in terms of flags and
borders and wallets. I know that if you and I were
offered the opportunity to go on the space shuttle
and go around the world for three days, we
wouldn't see flags; we would see a womb, and
we are all the babies. So let's get rid of this garbage
of borders and flags, because it only serves to perpetuate white supremacy over other people, as far
as I am concerned. I think that we need to teach
people the things that Bob Marley and Martin
Luther King were talking about. I went to the
mountaintop, and I saw the whole picture, and
there are no flags there. You know how at the
beginning of the Olympics every four years everybody is dancing and crying together and the flags
are just a wash of color — that is how it should be.

There is a lot to learn from the Native Americans about angels also. About certain principles. I
got really involved with them and, I tell you, out
of all the things I learned from Christianity and
from being with a guru from 1972 to 1981 learning about Eastern philosophy, I am finding out
that the cleanest and most spiritual water comes
from the Native Americans. There is no contra-
diction there. With the Christians and the Mus-
lims, there are contradictions — like how they
treat their women. In all our meetings, whether it
was Apache or Cherokee, from Canada to Brazil,

they say that their women always have the last word. This was coming from an old wisdom keeper and the way he said it made it clear to me that women have more of an ability to have compassion. We need to teach compassion. We all swing from the pendulum between good and bad. I think that there is another thing that we haven't tried, and that is pulling away from the pendulum. The first time I pulled away from being either good or bad was when I was in Japan and got very sick in 1981. I was so sick for three days that I had no energy to be angry or happy, and it was the first time I experienced true peace. I didn't have any energy to be good or bad. I thought, "Oh, you pull away from the good-and-bad pendulum, and here is compassion." I think that we haven't explored that one so much.

TERRY: I agree; I think it is time to go beyond good and bad, right and wrong.

CARLOS: Last year, after I read your books, I got attacked by depression and frustration. I woke up one morning in Cologne, and I was just depressed. I said, "God, everything is great. My family is great, my mom and dad have been together for over fifty years. What is wrong with me?" So I heard a voice say, "Take a shower and take a walk — get lost." And I said, "Okay." So I took a long walk, and in Europe they really have a thing about flowers and gardens. All of a sudden I was in front of a beautiful garden, and I was assaulted by purples and yellows, and I heard a voice that said,

"Stop and look at these flowers. The reason you are not happy is because you don't have gratitude in your heart. Flowers are put on earth to remind you what gratitude is all about. If you have gratitude, you will have happiness. If you don't, no matter who are you — Howard Hughes or Elvis Presley — you won't be happy."

TERRY: I think you are right; the two go together.

CARLOS: But gratitude has to come first. I felt so embarrassed, so I said, "I'm sorry, God, and it is just a human thing." I called my mom and I said, "Now I know why they say stop and smell the flowers; it is because of gratitude." If you can enter through the world of gratitude, you will cry tears of joy and you will say, "Thank you, God, for letting me breathe and participate in this thing of yours."

The last time I heard this voice was about two or three weeks ago. Someone called me from CBS records — and I am not there anymore — and said that Julio Iglesias wanted to record one of my songs, "Europa." And he would only record it if I played on it. Now you know, I am a street guy, and we have a thing about the system. I just don't get along with the system. I'm still a hippie, and I don't go for the straight thing. So I said, "Forget it; that is not going to happen." At dinner, I mentioned this to my mom. I said, "Julio Iglesias wants to record one of my songs, but he said he would only do it if I play on it, so I said forget it." I could tell by my mother's silence, which was really loud, that this didn't go over well with her, but she didn't say anything. So I went to play tennis after eating at her house, and I threw the ball up into the air to serve and the ball never came down. All I heard was the voice, which said, "Who gave you this song?" I said, "You did." And the voice said, "Well, why don't you let me do what I want to do with my song?" I said, "What do you want to do with your song?" And the voice said, "I want you to record the song with Julio, and all the money that you get from it, I want you to pledge it to the children of Tijuana. You don't need it." After this, I said, "Oh my God, okay." So I called everybody and arranged it.

To me, it is all a lesson in humility. I feel really good, because without this voice, the guitar wouldn't even stay in tune and people would go home. I have to be wise and follow the voice. It has gotten me this far.

TERRY: What do you feel creative success is?

CARLOS: Creative success is when you make people laugh and cry, and they accept a different reality about themselves.

TERRY: Did you have a spiritual turning point with your music, or have you always been connected spiritually to a higher power when you are playing?

CARLOS: I always knew that I had an impact on people. If they heard me playing on the street they would turn to see, and it wasn't the volume. But in 1967 and 1968, a combination of three people made me realize the universal questions. Mahalia Jackson,

Martin Luther King, and John Coltrane. They were the ones who said: Who are you? What are you doing, and for whom are you going to do it? And, I said, "I am a child of God, I'm a musician, and I am going to play for God." I learned a lot of things. I learned that all of us make a promise to the Supreme Creator before we come out of the womb. We say, "Lord, thank you for the opportunity. I promise to do my best to uplift, illumine, and transform the consciousness of humanity." That is the promise we all make.

TERRY: Do you think that our guardian angels know of that promise we made when we came into the world? And do you have one or more angels keeping you on your path?

CARLOS: I think there are a lot of them. It is kind of like one tree with many branches and leaves, but I think that the sap is the same. It is that sap that will help the tree go beyond forest fires and droughts and still give flowers. I tend to identify mostly with the sap, not the bark, as much as possible.

TERRY: When starting a new painting, a lot of painters say they try to clear their mind of old ideas and techniques and bring something new through. Do you do that when you are starting a new project?

CARLOS: Yeah. It comes in different ways. Sometimes you hear music so loud that you can't hear your wife or children talking to you. All you want to do is go in the studio and record the sound. It is kind of like when a woman is pregnant. Like giving birth — it has got to come out.

The Nature Kingdom

In the exciting buildup of angel awareness, I met an interesting traveler named Kip Davidson. Kip was a Celtic shaman who had a deep connection with the nature kingdom. We became very close friends and even though he lived in New Mexico and I lived in California, we shared many interesting adventures. One of my favorites was at an angel conference in Angel Fire, New Mexico. Dorothy Maclean, one of the founders of Findhorn, was there to present a workshop. Kip and I both regarded her as one of our spiritual heroes. A special moment came when a group of the workshop leaders met and we formed a circle to bring in the energies of the angels to lead us in the coming days of the workshop. I had no way of getting in touch with Kip by phone, and I knew he lived about two hours away. So I sent out a psychic call to him to join us at Angel Fire. I felt strongly he needed to be there. As the energy in the room was peaking, a ray of sunlight came through the skylight (it had been cloudy and rainy), and a beat later in walked Kip. The first thing he said was, "Sister, you have some strong medicine. I got the message and had to stop what I was doing and drive up here."

As a group, we went into the hills and Kip gave us an insightful tour of the devic presence that was all around us. I lost track of Kip after a few years. Then one day I was driving home and a deep sense of grief came over me. I started crying and crying, and I could not figure out why. I got home and cried for a while longer, then checked my messages. One of the messages was to inform me that Kip had crossed over. The caller knew we had been close and said that if I wanted to call and talk to her, I could. I thought, That is just like Kip! The inner message came before I knew what I was grieving over.

Following are some thoughts Kip shared in an interview with my friend Holly Phillips. The main topic was springtime.

KIP DAVIDSON

Most of us love the wind and the rain, the rivers flowing, the fire — the radiant heat upon our faces when we are out in the sun. The soft falling snow. And from that place of sweet love, the appreciation of this garden planet that we live on, we can go deeper and recognize our own divinity and our own humanity. From my experience, the angels, devas, and elementals bond to those people who live as much as they can through the difficulty of their everyday life in a place of sweet love and gratitude because this seems to be the vehicle that the devas and elementals live in. When we honor the divinity within ourselves and our own humanity, then the devas come out and recognize companions.

So beings here on schoolroom earth have been given the opportunity to express ourselves in creativity. When we join hands, figuratively speaking, in this prayer of gratitude, using these extraordinary tools that we have — our minds, our emotions, our physical bodies — and toil in the spring in our gardens with the angels, group vitality is brought back to the earth. This is because recognizing the devas and elementals of Nature is actually to remember a relationship that in our human history was once more intact than it is now.

During spring, one of the most fun things to do is to be still, anchored with our own Godhead — our own belief of Divine Source — and to listen in Nature. What we are listening for is very subtle and is often expressed as a feeling first, before an inner sound. The inner sound I am speaking of is a "signature" sound of the seeds as they are being planted. In handling the seeds with prayer and surrounding them with love and sometimes colored light emanating from our own auric fields, it is easier to build a bridge to hear the signature sound of the different seeds. In warmer climates, where the seeds have been in the ground for a while, we can hear the popping sound of this signature seed tone reaching a kind of a critical mass of expression and bursting out into the outer planes and moving up the soil.

At this time the devas take over, and they start building a pattern of harmony, of rhythm, which in time creates a critical mass of vitality. At that point, once this premanifest map of inner sound is created by the devas, the elementals come in, and they actually start growing the plant after this prepatterning from the high devas of Nature. This relationship between the devas and elementals tends to join the humans in singing to the plants and listening to the song of different plants and even the song of that "vital soup" that is the soil. Interpreting this inner sound with a poem and prayer and song allows us to join in the symphony of the new growth in our own garden. By doing this, we cocreate great vitality in our gardens, in our farms, and in our houseplants. It would be very visible if people chose to grow this way. There is no right or wrong. There is just love and gratitude and to intuit and allow the poetry and the song and the melody line to issue forth from our relationship with the plants.

I always feel that the devas are overlighting and premanifest builders of organic substance. Their relationship with the elementals, which can reach cosmic proportions, such as the relationship between the family of planets and stars, can be as important to spring as the microcosm, from our perspective, of this creative soup called *soil*.

I believe that the elementals and devas stem from a Creatrix — a God-Source of evolving opportunity. It's the dialogue or the dynamic relationship between humans and these devas and elementals that we emphasize as our human divine selves — as stewards here on the planet. It's very important that we recognize that we are managers here on schoolroom earth, because we have choice. We have just forgotten what that means. Devas and elementals need us just as much as we need them. Oftentimes we are as much of a myth to them as they are to us. The devas and elementals recognize in our energy fields that we are attempting to remember the sanctified purpose of our creativity in relationship with the Creatrix, with Gaia, with Earth. This does not have to be psychic, clairvoyant, or clairaudient, but simply the expression of love that we feel for our houseplants, our gardens, or our farms. The expression of love is the first and foremost vehicle for the relationship — and leads to the conscious recognition of this unyielding giving to the vitality and the evolvement of the planet. The devas and the elementals are reaching out to help us remember.

Devas understand the passions here on this water planet — a planet where we learn to love God. They

understand these difficulties and are oftentimes surrounding us during these moments of tearful sorrow or
joy in the garden with ether veils of colored light and
love flashes. Oftentimes our eyes wander and find a
particular part in the garden that seems to offer a place
of sanctuary for these private feelings of sadness and
expectation, of wholeness and remembrance of our
divine selves. And it is so simple just to be sitting there
amongst the companions that we have. They love us
because a hand is oftentimes involved in the growth of
gardens. Oftentimes they want to reach out and fill us
with love and compassion if we are in the wild, because
as soon as we recognize our divine purposes, the
quicker we will remember our relationship with our
divine selves, with the Creatrix, and with our lovely
planet, and reclaim our work joy and restore our balance so that the planet as well as ourselves can fully
realize a divine evolutionary potential. I suggest that
we take enough time to be still, sitting on the ground,
on the planet and surrounded by the plants, even if it is
in the snow, and be still until we can hear a response
from the elementals and the angels. They truly, truly
express great joy when we recognize that they love us.

Angels and Animals

My editor, Nancy Grimley Carleton, once again wrote a
powerful piece on animals and angels for my current book.
Since I have my own animal angel in the form of my angel
kitty, Guinness, I recognize the truth of her perceptions, and

I'm sure you will too (see the Resources section at the back of this book for Nancy's contact information).

NANCY GRIMLEY CARLETON, CALIFORNIA

I am sitting here in the shade of a magnificently gnarled oak tree elder at the U.C. Botanical Garden in the hills above Berkeley. A gentle breeze is blowing on this beautiful summer solstice day, and birdsong fills the air. Butterflies and hummingbirds dart by, drawn by the brilliant red and purple blossoms. Here, the angels remind me, is a taste of heaven on earth, always available if we open our eyes and our hearts.

When I had the honor of editing Terry's first book, *Messengers of Light*, she asked me to contribute a piece on animal angels. I wrote about my beloved childhood dog Tippy, and about Willow, a gray Netherland dwarf rabbit who touched my life with his presence between 1986 and his death in 1991. Since then, many other animal companions have graciously accompanied me on my path through this life. The unconditional love our companion animals give us offers an embodied experience of angelic love. A quotation from Meher Baba captures the quality of this love: "Those who do not have it catch it from those who have it. True Love is unconquerable and irresistible, and it goes gathering power and spreading itself until it transforms everyone whom it touches." The love and acceptance animals give their people doesn't end there; it fills us with the kind of love that spreads out to touch others.

Since my piece appeared in Terry's book, I have

received letters and calls from people around the world who have felt an angelic presence in their beloved dogs, cats, rabbits, and horses, among other animals. Because these animals truly come to be with us as an act of service, they are more than willing to do the angels' bidding and support us in becoming our highest, deepest, truest selves.

As the years have passed, messengers from the angelic realm have deepened my appreciation and respect for all the creatures on this beautiful planet. We have much to learn from the animals, and they thirst for us to see them for who and what they truly are: exquisitely sensitive beings who, like us, are here to love and grow and be. As I've made the process of connecting with animals a conscious part of my spiritual practice, I've had some amazing and deeply moving experiences with many of them, including squirrels, possums, frogs, rattlesnakes, owls, and even an alligator.

But for now I'm going to describe the evolution of my relationship with spiders (I asked for guidance about which animal I was meant to write about today, and the answer came in the form of a spider who appeared crawling on my dog Cinnabar's head while we were out for our morning walk). Spiders, of course, are animals that carry a distinct negative charge in Western culture — from the scary spiders in horror movies, to the wicked Shelob guarding Mordor in Tolkien's *Lord of the Rings*, to the constant references to finding Saddam Hussein hiding in his "spider hole." Our primal fear of spiders — relatively few of whom are actually poisonous to us — has all too often led us to lose sight of their beauty and power, and the many useful services they offer. On a mundane level, the number of spiders you see in your house may just be the exact number you need to keep your insect population from getting out of control!

Indigenous peoples around the world have recognized the powerful medicine the Spider People carry. The spider archetype is aligned with the deep feminine principle, which perhaps goes far toward explaining why our dominant culture vilifies them. Like Terry, I remember feeling frightened of spiders when I was a child (though I don't remember ever praying for God to get rid of them!), and I still have an instinctive dislike of spiders crawling on me. But for many years I have enjoyed magical moments in my encounters with individual spiders.

The first of these was an outdoor spider who somehow got inside and made a formidable web in the corner of our kitchen window. Since she seemed content to stay there and not wander all over the house, Susan and I decided to welcome her presence rather than moving her back outdoors. Every time we'd go down to the kitchen, she'd come out to say hello. She lived there for many months, and we enjoyed her greetings, which always spread good cheer. We named her Mrs. Spider, and grieved when she died, though we were touched that she left her body where we'd be sure to find it, ensuring that she became one of the few spiders to receive a full burial.

Some years later, a similar mottled brown spider

with a body the size of a large marble took up residence in the corner just outside a sliding glass door. She came out each evening to spin a lovely new web. Her presence was very strong, and she made it clear to me that she wanted to be called Cocoa. A shamanic counselor I consult with encouraged me to get her attention by singing to her. He said that spiders are willing and able to help human beings, but most of us have forgotten how to ask. By singing a song that honored her beauty and gave her respect, I established the relationship that enabled me to ask for her help.

With inspiration from the angels, a simple tune and lyrics came to me on a morning walk. Feeling a bit foolish at first, I got up a stepladder that evening to sing to Cocoa. Her response was electric in its intensity; I had definitely gotten her attention. She seemed to be drinking in the praise and respect I was showing her, and I felt her deep willingness to help in any way she could.

She soon helped me with a problem I was having with my dog Ginger, who was barking at night every time a possum or raccoon went by, which was quite often! I was desperate to quiet her swiftly so the neighbors wouldn't complain, and it was costing me quite a bit of sleep. On the nights when I remembered to ask Cocoa to weave a protective web of energy around the house, Ginger's barking subsided dramatically. You see, not only can spiders weave the physical webs we see glistening in the morning dew; they are also masters of creating energetic webs. I had recently been diagnosed with a rare and life-threatening autoimmune disease, and when I saw how effective Cocoa was at helping with Ginger's barking, you can be sure I asked her to help with my healing by weaving a web of energy and light around my body.

Our relationship deepened as fall turned into winter. A sudden and unusual cold spell that lasted nearly a month took an obvious toll on Cocoa, especially since it reduced the number of insects in her web. Despite being a squeamish vegetarian who never thought I'd be feeding a carnivore another living creature, I took to hunting moths and delivering them to Cocoa with a pair of tweezers. I am still moved by the exquisite delicacy she showed as she reached out ever so gently to take each moth from me — and by her obvious enthusiasm and gratitude as she wrapped it up and stored it in a little nook nearby.

Unlike the other outdoor spiders of her kind, Cocoa survived the winter; she finally left her body in the spring. Several weeks later, she appeared to me in a vision. I woke up with a jolt of energy one night and there on the pillow to my right was Cocoa, the same size but in a body made of light. She agreed to be one of my spirit guides and to live on my right shoulder. Since then I've had many dreams of spiders. Sometimes my task in the dream is to lie perfectly still while a spider crawls over my entire body; I have to be careful so I don't hurt the spider by giving in to the unconscious reflex to brush it off. These are deeply spiritual dreams and intimately connected to my healing.

I have received the assistance of many animals in the course of dealing with my illness, especially my beloved companion animals, including my beautiful golden dogs, my birds and hamsters, and the many rabbits who've been with me since Willow's death all those years ago. My rabbit Nutmeg chose to die in my arms to show me that death is truly nothing to fear.

With their help and the help of the angels, I am still here nearly six years after my diagnosis, and though I've had to change my life in profound ways, I am blessed to be one of the very few people with my disease who hasn't had to take the systemic prednisone and immunosuppressants that constitute the standard treatment (and which come with very serious side effects). I am deeply grateful for the love and support I have received from my angelic and animal friends and allies.

The angels can help us in opening up to direct communication with all of creation. I hope you'll join me in walking the path of connection with animals. I know it will bring you the kind of meaningful new relationships and magical synchronicities it has brought me.

The Place of Our Dreams

R. Buckminster Fuller said, "There is nothing in a caterpillar that tells you it's going to be a butterfly." I leave you with a poem written by someone who found his butterfly under very trying life circumstances. When we do our best and heed the call of the angels, we *are* all one in the light.

SOMETIMES

There is a space between the moon and the sun
Which nothing ever touches —
A space where the heart and the mind are born,
Unhampered by man's smallness, his possessiveness,
His fears, or his prejudices.
This is the place where all peoples meet as one.
Their light is the stars; their warmth,
The heavens around them.
Their hearts are connected as one,
And their minds are free.
All things live in the light, which is Love;
Its energy, understanding.
This is the place where time neither moves
Nor exists.
This is the place of our dreams.

— ALONZO LEON RHAMES

CHAPTER SEVEN

In the World, but Not Of It

*When Allah ordered the world, he spoke to the world, say-
ing, "World, the one who becomes your servant, treat him as
the worst of slaves. Beat him. Make him work hard and
when he dies, crush him. But if he becomes my servant, care
for him well and when he dies, hug him like a mother would
hug her child."*

— SUFI HADITH

I started out in the introduction to this book with a favorite
quote by Krishnamurti stating that truth is a pathless land,
which for me sums up the idea that we do not need an organization to be spiritual and grounded. I resonate with this principle,
but for me it came from knowing the organization first, in my
case, Christianity. I am truly grateful for learning to see the world
first through the eyes of Christian teachings. Looking back, I can
see that my first nineteen years centered around learning about,
debating, and discussing Christian teachings, and attempting to
live as a good Christian. I am grateful for the spiritual foundation
these experiences gave me, but I left the nest, so to speak, and
went out to find my own truth. One central theme that has
always stayed with me from Christianity is the idea that as spiritual folk guided by the angels, we are in the world, but not of it.

To keep things simple, let's say that the world here represents whatever takes us away from, or separates us from, our
devotion to God. Some of the things we can get hung up on
include greed, jealousy, violence, apathy, and the trouble that
arises from our attachments. Being not of the world means
different things to us at different moments in our lives. I feel
in my heart that it is an idea the angels want us to live with and
evolve with. The angels are not of the world in the physical

sense, but they guide us in making our physical times here meaningful and loving. Three questions come up when we think about "the world" as spiritual people: Do we renounce it, transcend it, or embrace it? For me it is a dance of all three.

The world promises us that our fulfillment will come through attaining certain things, such as money, prestige, fancy cars, and so forth. The spiritual dimension promises that our fulfillment already is, and that we can have money, prestige in the eyes of the world, and fancy things, but they are not the source of our happiness; without them, we would have the same level of love and happiness. That's the ironic deal we have with the world. The angels want us to embrace all that life has to offer, but with consciousness and nonattachment to worldly things. In our dance with life, we are tricked by illusion at times. The gift is not to get hung up on the trick, but to laugh at it — and know that ultimately everything is okay, perfect in being just what it is.

Being an "Optimystic"

When an interviewer once asked His Holiness the Dalai Lama how he could remain optimistic in the face of so much suffering and violence in the world, the Dalai Lama took a moment and then replied, "What would you suggest?" We may be asked a similar question about our own spiritual path at some point. Instead of explaining, justifying, or arguing, we can simply say from the heart that no matter what darkness befalls the planet, we are here to help the angels — and helping means to have faith, not fear, as our guideline.

It is also okay to be honest with ourselves and feel a lack of optimism at times, as long as we don't get stuck in that lack.

The angels teach us to be "optimystics" in our approach to life. This means sometimes we have to live with the "don't know mind," live with the mystery. Faith allows the "don't know" to be exciting because no matter what, we are letting the great Creator take care of things, and that involves trust. The choice is always ours — to trust in goodness or in doom.

I think we also need to get past the idea that death is a punishment. What I mean is that when world disasters happen, the focus of news reports is usually on the bodies of the "unlucky, unfortunate" people who met their demise. We are obsessed with extending life, but for what? What does marking time on this planet mean in the bigger scheme of things? We are here for a blink of God's eye, yet everything God does is important. There is no time in the angels' realm.

Some of the horrendous things my fellow human beings doing to one another are truly astonishing. I am not equipped with a processing device for most of it, so I put it in the category of "God's business" and go on doing my business — in the world but not of it.

Consider how you would be each day if:

- God spoke to you and told you that your main reason for being was to have fun and enjoy life.

- Each spark of life gave you deep reverence and gratitude, and the sense that being human is glorious.

- You saw God in every human face.

- The angels blessed you with true lightness of being.

- You were truly happy without reason.

- You were not allowed to worry.

What about Jesus?

Since my first book came out in 1990, I have received many letters from well-meaning Christians either condemning me or trying to "save" me from my wicked ways, because of the books I have written. The most common complaint is that I don't acknowledge Jesus as the only way to know angels, and that I don't refer exclusively to biblical scripture for my information on angels.

I was once interviewed for a Christian publication in an attempt to expose how damaging the current angel interest was to true Christians. The man interviewing me started out a bit arrogant, and then as we talked his arrogance vanished. He became very interested in how similar the miracles of Jesus were to some of the angel experiences people were having, and how angels were involved in people's hearts and lives changing for the better.

He then reversed his approach to the article and admitted to me that his original intent was to expose interest in angels as something bad, but now he realized there was no good reason to go after something that was helping people find God; this would only foster more separation when really the world is suffering from far worse things than good people interested in furthering their spiritual growth.

Christian author Ron Rhodes made a name for himself by writing a book in which he took sentences out of context from several popular books on angel consciousness in the attempt to prove what sinners the authors of these books were. I could take lines out of context from his Christian writings and do the same, but why bother? We don't need to go on and on criticizing others.

We are what we focus on, and what we give energy to expands. A great analogy is found in *The Serenity Principle* by Joseph V. Bailey, "[I]f you focus on the smashed bug on the windshield of your car, you will definitely miss the scenery and likely have an accident. Wisdom is like looking through the windshield, not at it." It takes a lot more wisdom and courage to connect rather than remove ourselves from life, projecting evil and wickedness onto others.

So, for the record:

1. I was raised and baptized a Christian. (I won't go into specifics.)

2. I have never doubted the existence of angels for a day in my life.

3. I was taught to end my prayers "In Jesus' name" (which I still do to this day).

4. I feel that Jesus represents the Christ consciousness.

5. I appreciate the Bible, and at the same time I think that it has been tampered with through the centuries. I think most of the "contentious" issues resulting from Christian beliefs originate with the apostle Paul's writings; I won't elaborate on my opinion in this book, but I mean to in the near future, probably on my website.

6. I do not understand why we all can't get along. At heart, all true light-centered spiritual beliefs have to do with making the world and the human heart lighter. Spending time taking apart other people's cosmology, in an attempt to expose them as dangerous, when they are good people

who believe in God, just doesn't make sense to me. There are real problems in the world, and if we as light workers unite and respect our differences, we can address what really threatens us.

7. My experience in the last twenty years with my own angel research project convinces me that 99 percent of the people who are attracted to angels are sensitive, compassionate, sensibly spiritual people who do not *use* angels as gods, or as replacements for God. I have no evidence that the angels help only those who believe a certain way. I do have plenty of evidence that the angels *respond* instead of *judge*, and that they do not base their help for humans on how religious those humans are. I do not think it is our job to protect the angels from misguided humans. If *we* were to try to manipulate the angels of light or dark with our forced sorcery, do you really think we would get away with it? Angels are not stupid. If we ask for trouble, we are going to get it. If we ask for the highest good and stay true to spiritual laws, we receive grace.

8. I make every attempt to understand where other people are coming from and to listen to their viewpoints, as long as they are not outright attacks. I can't help but let my beliefs color my writings, but I am not out to change anyone to my way of thinking. At best I want you to take what I have written and come up with new questions for yourself. One of the greatest things about writing is that only you can choose to

subject yourself to it. I can't force you to read something, and most bookstores will be happy to let you return a book you bought by mistake.

9. Most important, my personal relationship with Jesus is private to me; it is not something I care to argue about, or allow others to ruin because it doesn't fit into their belief systems.

What about Evil?

Separation is the devil's favorite avenue. The word *devil* comes from the origin of the word *slanderer*. The word origins for *diabolical* are *dia*, meaning across, and *ballein*, meaning throw. To throw across — to separate and slander, which is to lie — is the basis of evil, and I truly believe the lie of separation is what brings about most of our earthly problems. Things that cause fear create separation. And we fear what we do not know or understand.

When we separate ourselves from parts of humanity with a divide-and-conquer mentality, the results are the ills of racism, wars, injustice, and hatred. When we separate ourselves from what we know is right and true, and go after what is false and illusional, we cause an imbalance in ourselves. Our psyches split, and then our actions, thoughts, and intentions follow suit. When we separate ourselves from the earth by thinking that it is a big inanimate object to pillage and tame, we are missing reverence for life, ignoring one of the best ways to divinity: the beauty of nature. When we separate ourselves from God and the angels, we are separating ourselves from light. Reverence connects us and greed separates us; in the separation, contamination in the name of evil can infiltrate. Keep up a consistent flow of reverence and devotion in your life with help from the angels, and evil will have no room to get in.

WE ARE ONE

In the mid-1990s I had the privilege of facilitating a creative writing group at Juvenile Hall in the heart of Los Angeles, with the Inside Out program. My group was comprised of young men ages fourteen to eighteen, and we met as fellow writers. As a facilitator, I was not there to ask them why they were in Juvenile Hall, or to encourage them to write about their crime, unless that happened naturally. Also, everything written or said in the group had to remain strictly confidential. Once when we were discussing right and wrong, and punishment, and so forth, I told the group that many spiritual beliefs state that we are all connected, and that when something happens to an individual it affects the whole. This became a recurring topic of discussion, which they would initiate. Our conversations led in many directions, including the concept of karma, the spiritual law of cause and effect.

We had a powerful experience once after one of our writers served his time, went home, and then reappeared a few months later for killing a young man his own age, fifteen, with a gun. He wanted to come back into the writers' group, and on his first day back there was definite tension in the room. The other writers wanted to discuss the shooting. So I said, "Okay, to do this I am going to bring the young man who was shot back to life, and he is going to sit here among us, and we are going to ask him some questions about his short life." Then I said, "I will have the gun that shot him, and when I feel it is time I will hand the gun over to the shooter and he will have to kill him."

We asked our "visitor" questions such as "Do you have a girlfriend?" and "How do you kick it?" Of course, *we* were really the ones answering the questions, but we created a person who had a family, friends, and a future. Then it was time. I handed the imaginary gun over to the shooter, and said, "It's time to shoot him."

The shooter said, "I can't do it."

And I said, "Come on, kill him. He's right here next to you — your enemy. Do it."

He said, "No, I can't." When I asked why not, he said, "I don't know."

So I said, "I *do* know. Now you see that he is like you; we have made a connection with him that already existed — we just didn't know it. It was easy when you separated yourself from him and projected all your hatred on this stranger, but now that we know him and he is right here next to you, it's almost like killing yourself."

We went on to explore the ways we are all so similar at heart, regardless of our shape, size, neighborhood, religion, or gender. To separate from life promotes destruction; to connect to life as a whole allows us to respect, revere, and protect life. To do our best.

The simple request of the angels is that we stay connected to God and to the light, and to *behave* as connected human beings — revering and respecting life and our fellow humans. Love is a behavior, not empty talk.

A Note for Sensitives

The purpose of the world is for you to be lost in it, ultimately. The purpose of the world is for you to suffer, to create the

suffering that seems to be what is needed for the awakening
to happen. And then once the awakening happens, with it
comes the realization that suffering is unnecessary now. You
have reached the end of suffering because you have tran-
scended the world. It is the place that is free of suffering.

— ECKHART TOLLE

Have you ever thought that you are just too sensitive for life on earth? Have you thought that being sensitive is a curse? Well, it is actually a sacred gift. But it is difficult to cherish and protect the innate gift of sensitivity in a noisy and oftentimes offensive world. We can change the chemistry of our sensitivity into strength and personal power with the angels by our sides. Sensitives often take on more than they can handle because they sense the feelings of others and want to respond to them. Sensitives pick up the nuances of situations. It is as if the pain of others is screaming at them. And sensitives take too many things personally, things that really have nothing to do with them at all.

Jesus taught: "You are the salt of the earth, but if salt has lost its taste, its strength, its quality, how can its saltiness be restored? It is not good for anything any longer but to be thrown out and trodden under foot by men. You are the light of the world. A city set on a hill cannot be hid. Nor do men light a lamp and put it under a peck-measure but on a lamp stand, and it gives light to all in the house" (Matthew 5:13–15). Our sensitivity can be our greatness if we have the strength of God within us, or it can slowly drain us until we are of no use, like the salt spoken of in this quotation. The angels give us the strength to let our light shine and the wherewithal to overcome our fears of what other people may try to do to our light.

Each of us carries around a signature presence. Presence

is a matter of being in the present moment — meaning we are here now, awake and alive, being us. Presence is an authentic response to life. There is no way to lie to God in our prayers and in our actions. When we are authentic, we are our own authorities, and we become the original authors of our lives. This is where our personal power comes from. To feel powerful in life, as opposed to feeling victimized at each turn, we need to confront our sensitivity and personal responses, and strengthen our presence with God's love.

When we feel helpless in a situation with other members of our species, the best thing to do is to pray with our guardian angels. Our guardian angels are very willing to connect to other people's guardian angels and help the situation take a turn for the highest good of all. Just as we like to help others when a disaster strikes, our angels like to help one another too. So, if we send out prayers through our guardian angels, waves of love bless and change the situation.

We need discernment concerning when to help or get involved in other people's life issues. As sensitives, we have deep compassion and want to alleviate the suffering of others. This is truly a noble impulse, but it can end up causing more suffering if we are not careful. Rescue a victim, and you may become a victim of the victim. Help others too much with their careers, and you may rob them of the chance to make things happen on their own. When we try to make things happen for others, we rob the angels of the chance to help them be just where they need to be.

In certain aboriginal cultures, one of the worst offenses or crimes you can commit is dream stealing, which can be punishable by banishment from your tribe. An example of dream stealing would be if I were to tell you about what I want to create in the future, and you were to say, "Oh, there's no way you can do that" or "That is the craziest idea I've ever heard." Well, I'm sure you can grasp how prevalent dream stealing is in our culture, and there are certainly no laws against it.

I believe that there is another crime we commit readily in our society, and that is pain stealing. Pain is what teaches us and what gives us character; each time we try to ease other people's pain, we rob them of a chance to discover a message from their souls. This is a tricky concept, so it takes a great deal of thought and consciousness. I am talking here of emotional pain and suffering, which is so hard to deal with in ourselves and so hard to witness in others. But regardless of the situation, there are times when people need to honor their own pain, and the best we can do is to allow them the freedom to do so. Even and especially if others are trying to blame you for their pain, this is a signal to leave them on their own.

It is important that we understand the basics about energy. There are many ways to enter into energy problems with others. It helps to understand and recognize them so we can avoid them. When we seek to get an energy boost from other people, this means that some of their energy is going to come to us. Sometimes people offer up their energy to us by asking us for advice or help with a situation, and oftentimes this ends up draining us, or turning the tables, so to speak. The key is to know that all energy comes from the source of God; to recharge our own inner batteries with energy means going to God first and foremost.

Some people are agitators, and others are peacemakers. Sometimes it is difficult to recognize agitators because they are disguised as interesting or highly conscious people, who seem to be interested in the peace of all. Sometimes agitators may not even know that they have an agitating effect on others; how-ever, they probably know that they like to stir things up and that drama is somehow created around them. Agitators will drain us if we let them. It is our responsibility to recognize the feelings we get around others, and then to make the choice of how to handle this and personally respond while keeping in mind that we cannot control the behavior of those around us. *To agitate* means to disturb and cause anxiety. To know if others are caus-ing agitation in your life, think about how you feel after a simple discussion with them. How do they leave you feeling? Think about how *you* leave others feeling. At peace or in upset?

Most of all, it is important for sensitives to do the thing that is hardest for them: to think of themselves first, which in real-ity is thinking of God first. You have gifts that you are here to develop. No one gains when these gifts are wasted on futile attempts to save others, or when you feel bombarded by life. If we keep our inner flames healthy and strong, we will be able to ride the waves of tension and uncertainty to the shore of love. If we are out of balance, we may fall into the turbulent surf and flounder around. Keep yourself strong and powerful; you are shouldering a great responsibility in being a sensitive. You are part of a force fighting to keep beauty and love from becom-ing extinct on our planet. The angels are here to help, and God loves you. Your sensitivity is truly a gift when you pray often for discernment. Use prayer as your gateway to compassion. Whenever you feel the need to help another, pray in earnest first that the highest and most correct action be taken.

SOOTHE YOUR SENSITIVE SOUL

Here are some excellent ways to soothe your sensitive soul. Practice them often.

Music

Don't forget the cosmic dance, the language of the heart, the choirs of the angels. When you need an instant chemistry change, put on some beautiful music and let your soul dance and connect with that awesome love. Send it out to others. Beautiful music is immaculate prayer.

Rest

Get enough rest. Sleep isn't always restful. Think about true rest. Take restful naps when you need to. Go into your private space, and learn to take restful time-outs from the noise of life. Surround yourself in the peace of God by praying for deep rest. Allow God's love to hold you and melt away all your worries. Use angel alpha brain waves to center you.

Let It Be

In Virginia M. Axline's book *Play Therapy*, a seven-year-old boy is quoted during a session as saying, "Oh, every child just once in his life should have a chance to spill out all over without a 'Don't you dare! Don't you dare! Don't you dare!'" Have some fun and get messy!

Stay Inspired

If you lose it, meaning your balance or your perspective, do whatever it takes to get it back. Read a book, go to a movie, have dinner with a friend, send out a prayer, and above all remember to breathe. To inspire means to fill with the breath of God, the breath of life.

Change the Chemistry

Get outside once in a while, and I don't only mean outdoors. Get outside of yourself, outside of your beliefs, and outside of your routines. Some sanity accelerators in this regard include gardens, art, crafts, spiritual groups, nurturing pets — all positive ways we can lose ourselves.

What about Success?

I run into people all the time who are paralyzed
by the fact that they might fail.
To me, there's no failure. This is all an exploration.

— JOHN SAYLES

Who decides what makes some things successes and others failures? Are there really any failures? Calling something a failure is a judgment we make, usually based on comparisons. There is no true comparison to you; you are an original, and everything you do is successful if you choose to see it that way.

One way to choose spiritual success is to figure out what your values are — the things in your life that are the most important to you personally. When I worked with children in a human relations program, we would ask them to list their values, after we explained what values were. About 90 percent of the time, the top value on their lists was family. I found that wonderful. Other values high on their lists were love, education, pets, friends, home, school, community, hope, peace, and religion.

Make a list of your values. When you want to know if you are a success or not, look at your values and ask yourself if you have compromised them in any way. Compromising your values means you have not been true to yourself; you have created a rift in your consciousness. Sometimes we take the easy way out — or what seems to us to be the easy way — to achieve money or success. The easy way often goes against our values and against the highest good for all. Think about the times something didn't go right, and ask yourself if you were acting against your values. When you feel as if you have failed in some way, ask the angels for insight. Then forgive yourself, and look at what you can change to bring yourself into alignment with your core spiritual values.

What about Perfection?

Holy Spirit giving life to all life, moving all creatures,
root of all things, washing them clean, wiping out
their mistakes, healing their wounds,
you are our true life, luminous, wonderful,
Awakening the heart from its ancient sleep.

— HILDEGARD OF BINGEN

Something that is *perfect*, etymologically, is "completely made." The dictionary definition we are most familiar with is "without errors, flaws, or faults." *Perfect* also means complete and lacking nothing essential. Humans can get really hung up on the notion of perfection, but spiritually our imperfections are our spirit points of entry. It is said that the mystic visions of St. Teresa and Hildegard of Bingen may have come by way of migraine headaches. A broken bone can heal to be even stronger than regular bone tissue, and a broken heart is what eventually gives us our greatest strength.

In many cultures artisans purposely leave an imperfection as a place for spirit to enter their creations. For example, Amish quilters always make sure one patch doesn't match the rest in a finished quilt. They do this to remind themselves that the Creator does not make anyone "perfect." At Findhorn Garden, the gardeners leave a space to grow wild so that the natural spirit of the landscape can live without human intervention. I bought an Egyptian scarf at a fair once, with a fringe of beautiful purple beads. Scattered throughout were a few green beads, and the person selling me the scarf was happy to point out that these green beads were the spirit beads, where the spirit enters the garment to remind us that no one is made perfect. As the angel writer F. Forrester Church has pointed out, "After all, angels are not perfectionists. One was, of course, but he fell from grace."

These days, many of us are attracted to unusual items that are handmade or homemade, or that evoke the essence of coming from the heart and hands. When mass-market advertisers try to copy this essence with their slick ads, it just doesn't work. The mysterious "something more" that attracts us to specific art forms is not brought about by clean lines, digital editing, perfect pitch, and so on, but by something that speaks directly to our hearts — something we do not need to explain, exploit, or try to reproduce. It just is — "completely made" — and we are blessed when we recognize it. To allow the Holy Spirit to enter our lives, we need to love our imperfections, create from them, and proudly wear a green bead once in a while.

The Angels Say: Stay Awake and Love

I was regretting the past and fearing the future. Suddenly God was speaking. "My name is I Am." I waited. God continued.

"When you live in the past, with its mistakes and regrets, it is hard. I am not there. My name is not 'I was.'

"When you live in the future, with its problems and fears, it is hard. I am not there. My name is not 'I will be.'

"When you live in this moment, it is not hard. I am here. My name is 'I Am.'"

— HELEN MALLICOAT, LISTEN FOR THE LORD

There is no easy way out of life. If you choose to go to sleep and ignore life and love, then you will have nothing but disappointment and regret in your afterlife. I have always found it ironic that the people who have really lived and loved life have an easier time dying than those people who have lived in fear and bitterness and never enjoyed their time here. You would think that the people who love it here would hold on with the tightest grip, but this is not always the case. It is easier to leave a place when you know you have done your best. A good life springs from the roots of good *behavior*. It does not spring from envy or jealousy, or a sense of resentment because you think you aren't getting what you deserve or want out of life.

If you want to be loved, be willing to love. Find out for yourself what it really means to love well and freely, then take the risk. If you want to know if you are loved by another, ask yourself if you *feel* loved, and notice the behavior patterns. Love is shown, felt, and made visible in subtle and powerful ways. Love can be told, but if there is no action to back up the words, love has no vehicle. Words without love bounce off us and go out in the universe to be stored with the rest of our pretty words. Open all your senses to love. Ask the angels to help you keep your heart open, and you will be able to love, then love again, and then go out and love some more!

Wise Words to Contemplate

Friend, hope for the truth while you are alive.
Jump into experience while you are alive!
What you call "salvation" belongs to the time before death.
If you don't break your ropes while you are alive,
do you think ghosts will do it after?
The idea that the soul will join with the ecstatic
just because the body is rotten — that is all fantasy.
What is found now is found then.
If you find nothing now, you will simply end up with an
empty apartment in the City of Death.
If you make love with the Divine now, in the next life
you will have the face of satisfied desire.

— KABIR

May all that you learn here on earth bring you closer to the angels of love, light, and grace. You are blessed. You are loved. All that is truly required of you as a human is to have at least one sacred moment of real love. Then after the game, when you are asked, "How well did you love?," you'll have something to talk about in the locker room.

Acknowledgments

Someone wise once told me that a creative project begins as an embryo. At this stage, it is very fragile, and a pinprick (in the form of negative energy) can kill it. That is why we need to be especially careful about the people we have around at the beginning, and the energy they might project onto our ideas. As an idea gestates, it grows into the fetus stage, where it is less fragile but still needs protection to survive. Then comes birth itself, when the idea comes to fruition. Birth is a difficult process, but now the idea has life. Like any newborn, it needs guidance and nurturing to eventually make its way out into world.

In the embryo stage of this book, two people helped me tremendously: My angel cousin, Esther "Suzee" Williams, was not only very supportive; she saved me time and energy by typing many pages of text so I could weave them into place. Linda Kramer, my insightful and sensitive publisher, was the other proactive person during the embryo stage and throughout the fetus stage. She is truly a blessing in my life as an author. Our creative midwife was editor Nancy Grimley Carleton. She has worked with me on six previous book projects, and I was so happy to know that she would be guiding this book through its first breath. Working with Suzee, Linda, and Nancy couldn't have been better. I don't know how to thank them enough.

Now this book will go out into the world with the help of some really awesome people. Georgia Hughes, Kristen Cashman, Munro Magruder, and Kim Corbin of New World Library have great ideas and vision. Hal Kramer, founder of H J Kramer, and Marc Allen, founder of New World Library, are responsible for keeping the dream of light workers alive and well. Both of them are remarkable souls and self-realized in their own creative processes. I thank them for staying true to the big picture, and I am honored to be a part of it.

I have been extra specially blessed in this lifetime with wonderful friends and family who support me every step of the way. Jai Italiaander,

Shannon Melikan, Laurel Savoie, and Mary Beth Crain have been great friends for many years. Our experiences together have been the source of much inspiration. I thank them for the hours of laughter, love, and understanding we have shared.

As I noted in the dedication, my dad, Gordon Taylor, died while I was in the process of writing this book. His death took place on March 19, 2005, which just happens to be the feast day of St. Joseph, the patron saint of fathers. It is also Italian Father's Day. This departure date gave my sister Kathy and me a bit of comfort in the time of our loss, because we both felt that he was the ultimate dad. My father and my mother Nancy never faltered in their love for us, and they supported our creative endeavors even when these included beliefs not in complete alignment with their own. There is no way I can thank them enough. When my nieces Elizabeth and Jessica Godfrey were young, they would write little things for my earlier books, and they gave me all kinds of great information about the angels. They are now young women, and I am so proud of them. In a time of grief, several blessings have emerged. My dad's death brought me close again to my sister Kathy Godfrey, and to my Aunt Norma. Both have been a source of strength and love in ways that fill me with gratitude.

Ed Wortz was a hugely important influence on my adult life from the age of twenty-two on. He departed the earth plane right before I began this book. There are so many things that come up that I wish I could ask him about. His passing makes me realize how important good counsel is, and how blessed I have been in this lifetime to have known and learned from so many great people. He's right up there at the top of the list.

Thank you to my cheerleaders and muses: Peter Sterling, Amy Garcia, Li'l sis Cynthia Wootten Melendrez, Maggie Summers, Susie Eaton, Willie Campos, Katherine White, Shawn Davis, Joan Weldon, and Gerald Summers. Many thanks to Albert Valdez for the incredible painting that I kept near me as I was writing, and to Carolyn Mary Kleefield for inspiring me through the ether. And a special thank-you to the wonderful souls of chapter 6 for sharing their stories and their love.

Last but not least, I thank my husband, artist Rolo Castillo, for making me laugh, for sharing his unique perceptions of the world, for our love, and for just being. And thank you to our angel kitty Guinness for hours of delight.

Resources

All biblical citations are taken from the *Amplified Bible* (Grand Rapids, Mich.: Zondervan, 2001).

CHAPTER 1: MESSENGERS OF LIGHT

www.findhorn.org
Website for Findhorn Garden.

CHAPTER 2: ANGEL CONSCIOUSNESS

www.candacepert.com
Website of Dr. Candace Pert. This site provides information on Dr. Pert's research, as well as listing her lecture schedule.

www.thework.org
Website of Byron Katie. This site provides all sorts of great resources and information about Byron Katie and her method of personal inquiry, The Work.

www.whatthebleep.com
Website for the movie *What the #$BLEEP*! Do We Know!?* A lot of great stuff here, including interviews and ideas expanded from the movie.

www.masaru-emoto.net
Website of Masaru Emoto, author of *The Hidden Messages in Water*. This site provides further exploration of the mind-altering images of water

crystals. On this website Emoto provides water-crystal insight into current events happening worldwide, as well as listing his tour schedule.

www.InfiniteBeing.com

Website of Owen Waters. A great site for well-written articles on spirituality and physics/science, which will inspire you to think outside the globe.

CHAPTER 3: CULTIVATING RESONANT QUALITIES

www.innerlinks.com

828-665-9937

Website for the creators of ANGEL® Cards.

CHAPTER 6: TOUCHED BY THE ANGELS

www.centerfortruth.org

949-481-4040

Center for Universal Truth

27121 Calle Arroyo Ste. 2200

San Juan Capistrano, CA 92675

Website and contact information for the founders of Tara's Angels, Rev. Kirk Moore and Rev. Sandy Moore.

www.angel-guide.com

Lila*Star's website. This has to be my favorite site on angels — great spirit, fun, and good information.

www.iamchildrenofthesun.com

Savoie Faire Publishing

147 Carondelet St. #1059

New Orleans, LA 70120

Email for foreign shipping: sfpllc@aol.com

Laurel Savoie's website. Here you can get a preview of her wonderful book and CD, *Children of the Sun*. To order, send $39.99 plus $3.99 shipping and handling to the address listed.

www.harpmagic.com

Peter Sterling's website. The magical world of Peter and his harp.

www.arthurdouet.com

Arthur Douët's website. Many images of his work, with a great many angels.

Nancy Grimley Carleton

3044-B Halcyon Court

Berkeley, CA 94705

510-644-0172

Contact information for the editor of this book and six of my other books on angels.

OTHER RESOURCES

www.gilbertwilliams.com

The awesome art of Gilbert Williams.

www.thingsfromheaven.com

www.angelgift.com

805-648-5689, 888-ANGEL-17

365 E. Main St.

Ventura, CA 93001

Email: angel@thingsfromheaven.com

Contact information for Things from Heaven, a great angel site, and wonderful angel store.

www.dailycelebrations.com

A fun website offering much inspiration, good quotes, and a daily message.

www.deniselinn.com

Denise Linn's website. She is one of my favorite spiritual teachers.

www.angeltherapy.com

Doreen Virtue's website. She travels the world for the angels.

www.planetsark.com
The wonderful world of Planet SARK on a website.

www.alancohen.com
Alan Cohen's got a bead on all things metaphysical.

www.healthjourneys.com
Belleruth Naparstek's website. She offers some of the best guided imagery tapes for health, healing, and expanding one's intuition.

About the Author

$\mathcal{T}$erry Lynn Taylor grew up in and around the City of the Angels, Los Angeles. She just missed the cutoff date for being a bona fide hippie in the 1960s but was much influenced by her hippie elders, who helped usher in a new way of being, bravely clearing the path for the rest of us to explore the realms of consciousness in our own ways. She graduated from Old Dominion University with a bachelor's degree in psychology and has put in time toward a master's degree in mythology. In 1985, after years of spiritual investigation, she had an epiphany regarding the angels, which led to writing one of the first books to herald an era of grace and divine intervention from the angels, *Messengers of Light: The Angels' Guide to Spiritual Growth*. She currently lives in an arts colony on the edge of Los Angeles County with her husband and cat, hosting music salons and art openings.

Terry Lynn Taylor
website: www.terrylynntaylor.com or www.angelscanfly.com
email: 444angels@earthlink.net or
terrylynntaylor@gmail.com
Mailing address:
P.O. Box 265
La Verne, CA 91750

H J Kramer and New World Library are dedicated to
publishing books and audio projects
that inspire and challenge us to improve the quality
of our lives and our world.

Our books and audios are available
in bookstores everywhere.
For a catalog of our complete library
of fine books and audios, contact:

H J Kramer/New World Library
14 Pamaron Way
Novato, CA 94949

Phone: (415) 884-2100
Fax: (415) 884-2199
Or call toll-free: (800) 972-6657
Catalog requests: Ext. 50
Ordering: Ext. 52

Email: escort@newworldlibrary.com
Website: newworldlibrary.com